How to Create and Present

High-
Impact

Bible Studies

How to Create and Present

High-Impact Bible Studies

Elmer Towns

BROADMAN
& HOLMAN
PUBLISHERS

Nashville, Tennessee

0–8054–0169–5

Dewey Decimal Classification: 220.07
Subject Heading: BIBLE—STUDY AND TEACHING
Library of Congress Card Catalog Number: 97–40100

Unless otherwise noted, Scripture quotations are from
The New King James Version, copyright © 1979, 1980, 1982,
Thomas Nelson, Inc., Publishers.

Library of Congress Cataloging-in-Publication Data
Towns, Elmer L.
  How to create and present high-impact Bible studies / Elmer Towns
    p. cm.
Includes bibliographical references.
  ISBN 0–8054–0169–5
  1. Bible—Study and teaching. I. Title.
BS600.2.T68   1998
220'.071—dc21

                                                      97–40100
                                                          CIP

1 2 3 4 5   02 01 00 99 98

Contents

INTRODUCTION

Because the Bible is God's written message to us, it is important that we read and understand it. But many cannot make sense of the Bible and apply it to their daily lives. This book is written to help people study the Bible to understand its message. Then this book will help them go a step further: it will help them share its message with others. Therefore, this could be the second-most important book you've ever read because it will help you understand and teach the Bible—most important book in the world.

I think that every book I have ever written could be the most influential. Just as every mother dreams her baby will become the president of the United States or a great medical doctor, I dream that every new book will bless the world. This project is no exception. This much is sure: The church of Jesus Christ could be transformed if everyone learned how to study and teach the Bible.

This book was first a video project filmed in June 1996 for Gospel Light/Regal Books and released in the fall of that year. The video had eight lessons, each one designed to be used individually as a teaching tool in leadership meetings or together in an all-day training seminar.

These lessons are different than most books that tell you how to study the Bible. This book begins where they leave off with general principles of hermeneutics (principles to interpret the Bible). This book tells how to study different kinds of Scripture. Therefore, this will be a specific book to help you Study and Teach the Bible. *Study* and *teach* the Bible. You can see that in the outline of the eight chapters:

Ch. 1   Studying the Bible

Ch. 2   Studying a Biography

Ch. 3   Studying a Doctrine

Ch. 4   Studying the Bible Devotionally

Ch. 5   Studying Parables

Ch. 6   Studying a Chapter or Book from the Bible

Ch. 7   Studying a Story/Narrative

Ch. 8   Studying Prophecy

This book goes beyond Bible study. It will help you *teach* the Bible. Whereas most authors do not put together "study" and "teaching" in a how-to book, I felt it was necessary to put the two together. My definition of teaching first includes studying the Bible and, second, teaching the Bible.

Three Ingredients of Teaching

There are three ingredients to this definition of teaching. These three explain the uniqueness of this book.

> ### *DEFINITION OF TEACHING*
>
> *Teaching is the preparation and guidance of learning activities.*

Bible Teaching Ingredient #1: Preparation

1. Teaching is preparation. Recently I stood with two teachers in a preschool Sunday school class in my church. A little girl entered the room. One teacher excused herself, explaining that teaching began when the first pupil arrived. The second teacher said teaching began when *she* arrived in the classroom. While both ladies understood the necessity of preclass preparation, I felt their answer was inadequate. I didn't correct them because it would have been embarrassing in the circumstance. But teaching begins long before anyone arrives in the classroom. A teacher begins to teach when he or she begins to study and prepare the lesson. Therefore, this is a book about *how to study and teach the Bible.*

Bible Teaching Ingredient #2: Guidance

2. Teaching is guidance. The teacher cannot make pupils learn. All the teacher can do is *guide* the pupil through learning experiences. Learning is something pupils must do for themselves. There is an old saying "You can lead a horse to water, but you can't make him drink." This means a teacher can enroll a pupil in the class, but teachers can't make pupils learn. Maybe so! But teachers can put salt on their tongues so they'll want to

learn. The teacher can motivate pupils to learn by planning experiences, planning the sequence of experience, and planning for outcomes. This means the teacher is guiding pupils in learning experiences.

When going fishing in the North Woods, you need a guide. Without a guide, you may not get started properly, or you may not find your way, or you may not catch any fish. A teacher gets students started properly, guides class activities and helps students catch the fish of learning.

A teacher does not learn for pupils: the pupils must learn for themselves. A teacher guides the process.

There are two guides in Bible learning: the Holy Spirit and the teacher.

In a Christian context, the Holy Spirit guides us, helping us to learn the Scriptures. Jesus promised, "The Holy Spirit will guide you into all truth" (John 16:13). The Holy Spirit working through a human guide is illustrated by Philip helping the Ethiopian eunuch learn the Bible as they rode in a chariot. The Ethiopian had been reading the book of Isaiah but didn't understand what he was reading. Philip ran alongside to ask,

"Understandeth what thou readest?" (Acts 8:30).

The eunuch was returning from Jerusalem where he probably went to worship God. But he was blinded to spiritual truth and couldn't understand the Scriptures. The eunuch answered,

"How can I (understand) except some man guide me" (Acts 8:31).

The eunuch was asking for help to understand what he was reading. The human teacher must guide the thinking of pupils by explaining to them the basic content of the lesson. As they do that, the Holy Spirit removes spiritual blindness so the pupil understands the Bible.

This means the human teacher and the Divine Teacher must work together to produce learning when the Bible is taught. They are dual leaders in the learning process.

Bible Teaching Ingredient #3: Learning Experiences

3. Learning results from teaching experiences. Teaching is not telling: it is guiding pupils through experiences designed for their learning. Listening is not learning. When pupils experience the truth of God's Word, they learn its lessons.

Prayer

My prayer for you is threefold. First, may you better understand

WHEN STUDENTS EXPERIENCE THE BIBLE:

1. *They sense Bible discovery.*
2. *They experience self-activity.*
3. *They become interested and involved.*
4. *They feel the lesson solves their problems.*
5. *They work harder than before.*
6. *They cooperate with others.*
7. *They find that their needs are met.*
8. *They enter into the leader's experience.*
9. *They learn something new.*
10. *They enjoy learning and having fun.*

the Bible as you learn to study it. Second, may you learn how to guide your students in learning activities from the Bible. This is a prayer that you will be a successful teacher. Third, may your students learn how to study and teach the Bible. My ultimate success as an author will be measured by your success as a teacher. May God prosper our efforts and may many grow in the knowledge of the Bible.

Appreciation

Thanks to my long-time friend, Douglas Porter, professor at Canada Christian College, Toronto, for his help in research and preparing this volume from the videotapes. Also, thanks to my office staff, Linda Elliott and Amy Marston, for typing this volume.

May you discover many principles in the Bible as you learn how to study and teach the Bible.

Sincerely yours in Christ,
ELMER L. TOWNS

THREE STEPS TO BIBLE LEARNING

Each chapter in this book has three steps. STEP ONE gives you steps to understand the topic of that chapter. STEP TWO walks you through an actual study of the topic of that chapter. STEP THREE is a checklist for you to use in applying the steps of that chapter to other places in the Bible.

STEP ONE *These three steps are like learning to play golf. In STEP ONE you learn the principles by reading a book, viewing a video, or listening to an explanation.*

STEP TWO *In STEP TWO you take a club in your hand and actually swing it. You practice until a "swing" is developed. You learn to play golf, but haven't yet played golf.*

STEP THREE *In STEP THREE you go play a game of golf on a golf course. You put your principles and "swing" to work.*

Most books on Bible study and Bible teaching just tell you what to do. They're like teaching you to play golf by watching a video. Each chapter in this book will walk you through three steps so you will know and apply the principles of studying and teaching the Bible.

STEP ONE *This book will show you the principles of how to study and teach the Bible.*

STEP TWO *Next you will actually study the Bible by reading the verses and interpreting the passage.*

STEP THREE *Finally, each chapter contains a checklist to guide you in studying that topic.*

CHAPTER ONE

STUDYING THE BIBLE

Teaching the Bible is one of the greatest privileges available to the Christian. A Sunday school teacher explaining a Bible story to a group of young children is communicating a message that will influence them for a lifetime. The Bible study group leader guiding a discussion in a comfortable living room is helping people discover God's answers to the pressing questions in their lives. Those who teach the Bible are investing their lives in a ministry with eternal results. Only two things last forever, the Bible and people. Therefore, when we help people understand the Bible, we influence eternity. We communicate the eternal Word of God to people who will live forever.

One of the best known biblical preachers of this century is Dr. W. A. Criswell, who pastored First Baptist Church of Dallas, Texas, for almost fifty years. Over a period of thirteen years, he preached through the entire Bible, passage by passage, beginning at Genesis 1:1

and ending at Revelation 22:21. Early in his ministry he became convinced that the best investment of his ministry was to teach the Bible to his people. The success of his ministry in Dallas, Texas, suggests his conclusion was accurate.

Five Rules of Biblical Nutrition

The study of the Bible is foundational to one's growth as a Christian. Therefore, every Christian should plan to study the Bible, much as one eats food to grow physically. Actually, several parallels may be drawn between good eating habits and a healthy approach to Bible study.

1. *Eat enough.* Eating too much or too little food has long term implications on both the body and spirit.

2. *Eat a balanced meal.* Just as one does not grow strong physically by eating only desserts, so a Christian will not grow strong in the faith without a balanced approach to Bible study.

WHY TEACH THE BIBLE?

The life of God is in his Word; the Word is quick and living (Heb. 4:12–13). The Word of God is a mirror (James 1:23); it reveals to us our true selves. The Word of God is a seed (Luke 8:11); it contains the life and vitality of the Lord. The Word of God is a sword (Eph. 6:17); it pierces the heart and lays bare and naked our sinful souls before him who only can save us from death. The Bible is a life-giving Word (1 Peter 1:23); it is the vehicle for imparting that life to us which is in Christ Jesus the Incarnate Word. Eternal life for the individual soul begins through believing the testimony of God.[1]

1. W. A. Criswell, *Why I Preach That the Bible Is Literally True* (Nashville: Broadman & Holman, 1995), 24.

3. *Savor your food.* Don't just stuff your mouth or swallow without chewing. You need to both devour and digest the Scriptures as you study.

4. *Avoid a constant diet of junk food.* We must eat healthy food and avoid a constant diet of party food. Many Christians get sidetracked in their Bible study by becoming involved in speculation and meaningless side issues, such as prophecy or an endless study of numbers.

5. *Eat with dignity.* We should eat with dignity, not like a dog or a pig. One way to accomplish that goal is to eat routinely rather than only when you want to eat. Eat-

> *The secret of our future lies in our daily routine.*

ing balanced meals at regular intervals is one key to long-term good health. Likewise, getting into the Scriptures on a daily basis is a good discipline to encourage ongoing spiritual growth. The secret of our future spiritual maturity lies in our daily routine of Bible study.

Ten Things Bible Study Will Do For You

The Bible is a book about God. It is not just history with references to God's people, nor is it a record of poetic songs of religious people. The Bible is a book about God. It is not just a book about the birth, life, and death of God's Son, nor is it just a story of the subsequent spread of Christianity. It includes all these, but it is a story about God, given to us from God, written by God through His servants a story that points us to salvation and worship of God.

The Bible is God's revelation of Himself to you. When you understand this principle you begin to understand the Bible. Since God is who He is, then what is true of God must also characterize the Book that describes Him. God is the Source of this revelation (Deut. 29:29). Christ, the Son of God, is the central theme of the Bible (John 5:38). The Holy Spirit is the divine Author of Scripture (2 Pet. 1:20, 21). Therefore, the Bible is the revelation of God, Christ is the message of the Bible, and the Holy Spirit is the author of the Bible.

The Greek word *inspiration,* that Paul used to describe how the Bible was written, literally means "breathed-out from God." "All scripture is given by inspiration of God" (2 Tim. 3:16). Jesus spoke of "every word that proceeds from the mouth of God" (Matt. 4:4). Therefore, when you pick up the Bible to study its pages, you have God's book in your hands. Determine to get God's message into your mind.

1. *Personal Bible study will strengthen your Christian life.* The Bible is your source of strength in your Christian life. John wrote, "I have written to you, young men, because you are strong, and the Word of God abides in you" (1 John 2:14). As you consistently study the Bible, you will be strengthened to meet the challenges you encounter in life.

2. *Personal Bible study will strengthen your assurance of your relationship with God.* In the same epistle John also wrote, "These things I have written to you who believe in the name of the Son of God, that you many know that you have eternal life" (1 John 5:13). Christians who tend to struggle with the assurance of their salvation also struggle with the discipline in personal Bible study.

3. *Personal Bible Study will strengthen your confidence in your relationship with God.* According to the Apostle John, "This is the confidence that we have in Him . . ." (1 John 5:14). Our assurance comes from God to us through Bible study.

4. *Personal Bible study will undergird the effectiveness of your prayer life.* Bible study is an important key to getting answers in prayer. You get answers when you come to God by the Bible. Jesus told His disciples, "If you abide in Me, and My words abide in you, you will ask what you desire, and it shall be done for you" (John 15:7). This promise extends beyond those gathered in the Upper Room that evening. It is a promise to be claimed by every Christian involved in the discipline of personal Bible study.

5. *Personal Bible study will help you overcome sin.* The Bible describes itself as "profitable for doctrine, for reproof, for correction, for instruction in righteousness" (2 Tim. 3:16). As you study the Scriptures, you learn doctrines which are the principles of Scripture to govern the way a Christian should live. Occasionally, these principles reveal how you live contrary to God's way. Therefore the Scriptures correct the wrong way you live and instruct you in the correct way of righteousness. As you respond to this ministry of

- Learning doctrine,
- Learning reproof,
- Being instructed in righteousness,

you deal with sin in your experience. Jesus told His disciples, "You are already clean because of the word which I have spoken to you" (John 15:3).

6. *Personal Bible study will bring you internal joy.* Jesus assured His disciples, when He said, "These things I have spoken to you, that My joy may remain in you, and that your joy may be full" (John 15:11). Joy comes from Jesus' words.

7. *Personal Bible study will bring you peace.* Jesus promised His disciples peace when He added, "These things have I spoken to you, that in Me you may have peace" (John 16:33). Therefore, peace comes from Jesus' words. The joy of the Lord and peace of God are two experiences that come from the Word of God planted in your life.

8. *Personal Bible study will help you make good decisions.* The Psalmist observed, "Your word is a lamp to my feet and a light to my path" (Ps. 119:105). The principles you learn through the daily study of the Scriptures will guide you through the issues involved in each decision you make. Many Christian business-men have developed the habit of reading one chapter from Proverbs as they begin each day. They read the entire Book of Proverbs once each month by reading one chapter a day. As they make decisions throughout their business day, they do so with the added advantage of God's wisdom to help them eval-uate each situation they face.

9. *Personal Bible study will help you explain your faith to others.* The apostle Peter urged Christians, "Sanctify the Lord God in your hearts, and always be ready to give a defense to everyone who asks you a reason for the hope that is in you" (1 Peter 3:15). The better you understand the Bible, the easier it will be for you to explain the message of the Scriptures to others. Those who are most effective in sharing their faith with others

are those who have gone one step further in their Bible study. As they come across verses which summarize the teaching of Scripture on various subjects, they commit these verses to memory to be used in later conversations about their faith.

10. *Ultimately, personal Bible study leads to success in every aspect of your Christian life.* The word "success" occurs only once in Scripture and it is found in the context of meditating on the Scriptures. God promised Joshua, "This Book of the Law shall not depart from your mouth, but you shall meditate in it day and night, that you may observe to do according to all that is written in it. For then you will make your way prosperous and then you will have good success" (Josh. 1:8). Many successful Christians have prove God honors this promise, by giving priority to personal Bible study in their lives.

How to Get a Hand on the Bible

As a young minister, I was called to the home of Mrs. Van Brackle late one evening. She was 82 years old and partially blinded with cataracts. She had been told her lack of faith kept her from being healed. She asked me, "How can I get more faith?"

It was a question that intimidated me. At first I didn't know how to answer the question. Then God brought a verse to mind that answered her question: "Faith cometh by hearing, and hearing by the Word of God" (Rom. 10:17 KJV).

"The more you get the Bible in your life," I told Mrs. Van Brackle, "the more faith you will have." I told her she could have strong faith if she learned the Bible, obeyed the Bible, and let the Bible fill her life.

"You have to get a grip on the Bible to get a grip on faith," I explained to this elderly woman who was looking for a touch from God.

I held my hand out toward Mrs. Van Brackle to show her five fingers. Then I told Mrs. Van Brackle, "It takes five fingers to get a strong grip on the Bible." Then I held my Bible with all 5 fingers.

I explained, "Holding the Bible with one finger" is not enough. Then I compared one finger to using only one method to get hold of the Bible. Then I went through an exercise of holding the Bible with one finger . . . two fingers . . . three fingers . . . four fingers, and finally I demonstrated the strong grip I had on the Bible when I used my entire hand to hang on to the Bible. Then I explained to her, "There are five things that will help you get a grip on your Bible."

> ### WHEN TO STUDY THE BIBLE
>
> 1. *Study when you are physically alert. (Some in the early morning, others late at night).*
> 2. *Study when you are not interrupted.*
> 3. *Study when you can focus on the Scriptures.*
> 4. *Study a little each day (forget about spending all day in the Word).*
> 5. *Study immediately before teaching (before taking an exam, study all semester, but review before the exam).*

1. The First Finger—Hear. You begin Bible study by attending church where you hear the Word of God taught and preached. This includes both the public reading of Scriptures and explanation of Scriptures. Paul reminded the Romans of the source of their faith, "So then faith comes by hearing and hearing by the word of God" (Rom. 10:17). Hearing the Scriptures will lay a foundation for all future Bible study.

2. The Second Finger—Read. We should read the Scriptures for ourselves. This does not only mean public reading, it also includes private reading. Paul told Timothy, "Till I come, give attention to reading, to exhortation, to doctrine" (1 Tim. 4:13). You read the Scriptures to understand them. In the early church, many people were illiterate. As a result, the public reading of the Scriptures was an important part of the worship service. The last book of the New Testament promised a special blessing upon those who read the Scriptures. "Blessed is he who reads" (Rev. 1:3). Many Bible teachers believe that promise can be applied to all who read the Scriptures in church assemblies and privately for themselves. But when we read the Scriptures, we should follow the advice Mark gives to those who read the Scriptures: "Let the reader understand" (Mark 13:14).

3. The Third Finger—Study. Studying involves getting a firm grasp on the Scriptures by diligently investigating the Bible for ourselves. Paul urged Timothy, "Study to show yourself approved unto God, a worker that needeth not to be ashamed, rightly dividing the Word of truth" (2 Tim. 2:15 KJV). Many people find marking or underlining their Bible helps them in their study. Others like to write notes in the margin of their

Bible as they engage in personal Bible study. Of course, the real value of Bible study is not the marks you make in your Bible but rather the mark the Scriptures make in your life.

4. The Fourth Finger—Memorize. It is important to commit portions of the Bible to memory in Bible study. The Psalmist testified, "Your word have I hidden in my heart, that I might not sin against You" (Ps. 119:11). One man who recognized the truth of this statement was the nineteenth century evangelist D. L. Moody. Moody had written in his Bible, "This book will keep you from sin, or sin will keep you from this book." Memorizing portions of Scripture will help us overcome temptation just as the Scriptures were helpful to Jesus as He was tempted by the devil (Matt. 4:4, 7, 10).

5. The Fifth Finger—Meditate. Investing time meditating on the Scriptures will help internalize the truth of God so that biblical principles become a part of your normal thought patterns. One mark of the man or woman of God is "his delight is in the law of the LORD, and in His law he meditates day and night" (Ps. 1:2). Each of us has four times in a typical day when we can devote time to meditating on Scriptures we have learned: "When you sit in your house, when you walk by the way, when you lie down, and when you rise up" (Deut. 6:7).

Practical Helps

The Bible is a big book. Actually, it is a collection of sixty-six books containing 1,189 chapters and 31,175 verses. Like exploring the Canadian North Woods, the Bible is so big you would get lost if you didn't have a plan to guide your study. If you begin the discipline of personal Bible study without a plan, you could become overwhelmed. You might get discouraged and give up, or you might end up chasing rabbits on rabbit trails that lead nowhere. As you proceed through this book, you will discover several approaches to Bible study as you consider teaching different expressions of truth from the Bible. At this point in your study, it would be good to consider a few preliminaries which apply to each approach to Bible study.

As you personally study the Bible use a pen or pencil and paper. Write as you study.

Someone said, "You don't have a thought until you can write it down." So write out your insights and findings. Don't rely on your memory.

> *A short pencil is better than a long memory.*

As we study the Scriptures, we will gain various insights into the meaning of verses on the character of people. By writing out these insights on paper, you preserve them for future use. When you get ready to teach, review all of the notes you have written, organizing them into a lesson plan. Do not try to teach a lesson from the notes you make each day. Again, you will want to write your study notes into a lesson plan.

Keeping notes of your Bible study not only assists you in remembering what you have learned, it also helps the learning process. You don't really understand your thoughts until you express them in words.

> *Thoughts disentangle themselves over lips and fingertips.*

As you attempt to explain an idea to someone else or record an idea on paper, you must first clarify the idea in your own mind. Many teachers attempt to write the key thought from their Bible study in one or two lines as a first step before attempting to share that truth with others in a lesson.

How to Study the Bible

Years ago I began my Bible study with four questions. These were given to me by a mature Christian who was mentoring me in Bible study. I didn't have a real plan by which to study, so these four questions gave me a specific daily plan to Bible study.

1. What is the point of the passage? A key to effective Bible study is to focus on the main point of the passage. It is easy to become sidetracked by looking into insignificant details. When you do that, you usually

> 1. What is the POINT of the passage?
> 2. Where is this thought found in PARALLEL passage?
> 3. What are the PROBLEMS in this passage?
> 4. What are some PRACTICAL applications for this passage?

miss the whole point of a passage. Even some Bible teachers have become sidetracked on matters like the number of details in Noah's ark and missed the whole point of God's saving purpose in providing the ark for Noah and his family during the flood.

As you study the Bible, you need to constantly ask the question, "What is the point of the passage?" Most students of the Bible find there is far more truth to be gleaned from the Scriptures when Scriptures are allowed to speak for themselves, than when you go looking for things that are not there, or things that really are not that important.

2. Where is this thought found in a parallel passage? To make a passage of Scripture come alive, begin by attempting to write out the point of each verse in the chapter. If it is a story, write out the point of the story. Why is it in the Bible? The second step in your study of a biblical passage is to ask, "Is there another description of this event somewhere else in the Bible?"

Each gospel describes the Feeding of the Five Thousand, but each time the miracle is recorded, there is a different emphasis. We gain a more complete understanding of what happened when we read all four descriptions of the miracle.

The New Testament sometimes refers to Old Testament events. As you read and study both, you gain insight into the passage before you teach it.

As you look for parallels, also search for verses that teach the same principle or give additional insights on the same issue. Peter explained the reason for this approach to Bible study when he wrote, "Knowing this first, that no prophecy of Scripture is of any private interpretation" (2 Peter 1:20). No thought of Scripture stands alone; it will be reinforced at other places in Scripture. Therefore, the Bible describes the process of comparing Scripture when it directs us to "Compare spiritual things with spiritual" (1 Cor. 2:13). The word *private* means we interpret Scripture in fellowship with other believers. The Holy Spirit has only one meaning, and we are to find His interpretation of the Scriptures. If you have a private interpretation different from every other believer it's probably wrong. Another way to study using the parallel approach is to look for ways key words are used in other Scriptures or look for similar events in the lives of different people.

3. What are the problems in this passage? Solving problems can also be an important part of your Bible study. You often learn most when you are motivated to solve a significant problem in your life or the life of someone close to you. Therefore, as you begin your Bible study, take time to clarify the problems you find. Write them down. List problems whose solutions are obvious to you, for these problems may be an obstacle to someone else. Problem solving is an effective way of teaching. As you suggest solutions in class, you may help someone else. Begin by writing out the problems that are easy and then those that stump you. You probably will not solve a problem until you first clarify it by writing it down.

4. What are some practical applications from this passage? Personal Bible study should always be practical. James urged his readers, "But be doers of the word, and not hearers only, deceiving yourselves" (James 1:22). The ultimate goal in our Bible study should be the discovery of principles by which we live our Christian life. Not only should you record your Bible study notes, you need to also write out the way you intend to apply the Bible in some specific context in your life.

The first step in applying the Scripture is to pray and ask God for help. Actually, you will want to pray for three things. First, you will want to pray for the Holy Spirit to teach you the lesson you are studying. "When he, the Spirit of truth is come, he will guide you into all truth"

Prayer Preparation

Pray for the Holy Spirit to teach through you.

Pray for your preparation.

Pray for your pupils.

(John 16:13). The Holy Spirit can take away your blindness and help you understand the Bible. Second, ask God to help you in actual lesson preparation. You will want divine help in arranging your lesson plan. Finally, pray for your students. Ask God to help them learn and apply the lessons you will teach.

God has given us a revelation of Himself in the Bible. He did not give it to us to frustrate us with something we could not understand. So, God intends for us to understand the Bible and learn from it. God also gave each Christian the Holy Spirit to illuminate the Scriptures, so that the message of God could be understood. As we study the Bible, we need to apply sound principles of interpretation.

Learning from the Bereans

The Berean Christians' model for us is a good approach to personal Bible study. "These (Bereans) were more fair-minded than those in Thessalonica, in that they received the word with all readiness, and searched the Scriptures daily to find out whether these things were so" (Acts 17:10).

The first description of the Berean Christians suggests they were yielded to God in their approach to the Scriptures. They "received the Word." As we approach Bible study, we also need to do so on the basis of being willing to receive and apply any and all biblical principles found in the Scriptures.

> **Prayer**
>
> *Lord, I will receive and study Your Word. I receive the Bible from You and will reverently study its meaning. Amen.*

Second, the Bereans were intentional in their approach to Bible study. They came to the Scriptures "with all readiness," looking for truth. They had an eager mind, also described as a hungry spirit. It was not a matter of reading a chapter to fulfil their Christian duty but rather a desire or pursuit of a better understanding of the truth of God.

> **Prayer**
>
> *Lord, I love Your Word and want to know it better. But since I'm human, and have limited understanding, be my teacher. Give me a deeper hunger to know You by studying the Scriptures. Amen.*

In the third place, the Bereans approached Bible study with a word-by-word study of the Scriptures. They "searched" the Scriptures in their pursuit of truth. Theirs was not a superficial reading, but digging into the

> **Prayer**
>
> *Lord, I commit myself to study to understand your words and may I grow to maturity. Amen*

meaning of words. The word *searched* means "sift" as a baker sifting flour to separate each particle from every other particle. When you study the Bible "word for word," you are "sifting" every particle of Scripture to make you understand what God is saying. As you invest time looking up the meaning of words and expressions used in Scripture, you gain insights missed by those who gloss over details in their study of the Scriptures.

The fourth characteristic of the Bereans was their routine of "daily" Bible study. Each day these Christians had a fresh encounter with God through their study of the Scriptures. On a daily basis they were reminded of God's merciful compassion toward His people (Lam. 3:22, 23). Just as Jesus instructed His disciples to pray for daily bread (Matt. 6:11), so we need to go daily to the Scriptures which are the Bread of Life to the believer.

> **Prayer**
>
> *Lord, I commit myself to daily Bible study. Give me discipline to study and learn more about You. Amen.*

The fifth characteristic of the Bereans was their purpose in Bible study. There was something the Bereans wanted to know as they came to the Scriptures. They studied "to find out whether these things were so." This verse tells us they were concerned with content and assurance. They wanted confidence from their Bible study. Likewise, we would be wise to follow that example in our own Bible study.

> **Prayer**
>
> *Lord, help me focus my investigation so I can know exactly what You want me to know and what You want me to do. Amen.*

When we study the Bible, we are looking for the content of a message from God. We want a message that can be trusted. With that attitude, we want confidence in what we hear from God. Ask God to open your eyes and give you insight into what you read. The Psalmist prayed, "Open my eyes, that I may see wondrous things from Your law" (Ps. 119:18). If sin is hindering your relationship with God, it should be confessed to Him that you might be cleansed (1 John 1:9). Then as you read, you need to listen carefully to what

God is saying to you (1 Sam. 3:10). Even as you begin, you need to be prepared to obey what God tells you through your personal Bible study (Acts 9:6).

Getting Ready to Teach

The goal of your personal Bible study is not merely the acquiring of new knowledge, neither can it be limited to the benefits you realize in your own life. The ultimate aim of your personal Bible study is to share insight with others and see the Scriptures change their life.

Paul urged this twofold action on the Colossian Christians: "Let the word of Christ dwell in you richly in all wisdom, teaching and admonishing one another in psalms and hymns and spiritual songs, singing with grace in your hearts to the Lord" (Col. 3:16). Just as the principles you learn in your Bible study help you grow, so you can help others experience significant spiritual growth in their lives as you share what you are learning with them.

Therefore, teaching the Bible is your goal in personal Bible study. Teaching is the means by which you help others learn what you have learned in your Bible study. But remember, teaching is not talking, and learning is not listening. Learning is actively being involved with the Bible. With this in mind, I have defined teaching as "the preparation and guidance of learning activities."

Simply surveying the Scriptures is not Bible study, nor is it Bible teaching. Many teachers do this in their Sunday school class or home Bible study. They think they are teaching or leading a Bible study because they fill a classroom with talk. But you have not taught until your pupil has learned, and the real key to learning is active involvement. Therefore, teaching involves "learning activities."

How you study determines how you teach. Therefore, you must become actively involved with the Word of God as you study. Then you must guide your students to become actively involved in your teaching process.

The real role of the teacher is that of a guide. That was Philip's role as he taught the gospel to the Ethiopian eunuch. He began by asking the eunuch, "Do you understand what you are reading?" (Acts 8:30). The eunuch did not understand the text and knew that he was having difficulty understanding the Scriptures. He responded to Philip's question with a question of his own: "How can I, unless someone guides me?" (Acts 8:31). The eunuch used the word *guide* as a synonym for *teach*. He was asking, "How can I understand the Bible except someone teach me."

Human teachers cooperate with the Divine Teacher to change lives. Jesus told His disciples, "But the Helper, the Holy Spirit, whom the Father will send in My name, He will teach you all in My name. He will teach you all things, and bring to your remembrance all things that I said to you" (John 14:26). The Holy Spirit is the Divine Teacher, but He is also a guide. Later that same evening Jesus added, "However, when He, the Spirit of truth, has come, He will guide you into all truth" (John 16:13). The Holy Spirit is the real teacher in your Sunday school class or Bible study group. Your teaching is most effective as you cooperate with the Holy Spirit in teaching what He wants taught during each session.

> **Prayer**
>
> Lord, I yield myself to You so I can learn Your Word and grow in grace. Teach me everything I need to know. Then fill me with the Holy Spirit and teach others through me. Amen.

Tools for Bible Study and Interpretation

I have not attempted to list all the Bible study tools available, but only those that have been the most helpful in my study. The annotation is personal; I have commented where the tool helped me.

LaHaye, Tim. *How to Study the Bible for Yourself.* Eugene, Oreg.: Harvest House, 1976. Practical lists with good study helps and charts. This is the one I recommend first to a new believer.

McQuilkin, Robertson. *Understanding and Applying the Bible.* Chicago: Moody Press, 1983. Dr. McQuilkin was my theology teacher at Columbia Bible College, where I appreciated his love and commitment to God's Word. This book has more on interpreting the Bible than studying it.

Pierson, Arthur T. *Knowing the Scriptures.* London: James Nisbet and Co., 1910. I learned a "heart hermeneutic" from this book. It gives the overflow of a lifetime of studying the Bible, including principles that only the knowledgeable student will appreciate and understand.

Pink, Arthur. *Interpreting the Scriptures.* Grand Rapids: Baker Book House, 1972. Dr. Pink's written sermons are among the best in interpreting and applying the Bible. This book has been one of my reliable tools for help in lesson preparation. Not a book on Bible study but interpretation.

Smith, Wilbur M. *Profitable Bible Study.* Grand Rapids: Baker Book House, 1963. (First appeared in 1939.) Dr. Smith taught with me at Trinity Evangelical Divinity School, Deerfield, Illinois, where his love and warm application of the Scriptures attracted large classes. This book shares eight basic Bible study techniques and ways to apply them.

Thomas, Griffeth. *Methods of Bible Study*. Chicago: Moody Press, 1926. Most of the book gives the results of Bible study. A summary of Bible topics for the average believer and how to study the Bible to arrive at these doctrines.

Traina, Robert A. *Methodical Bible Study*. New York: Ganis & Harris, 1952. This is a foundational book for all the methods of study in this volume. The author teaches how to observe Scripture, interpret it, and apply it to life. This was the foundational book I used at Dallas Theological Seminary.

Wald, Oletta. *The Joy of Discovery*. Minneapolis: Bible Banner Press, 1956. This is one of the few books that ties Bible study to Bible teaching. Excellent on inductive study.

Studying the Bible Approach the Scriptures

1. What two things does the Bible claim for itself?

   "All Scripture is given by inspiration of God, and is profitable for doctrine, for reproof, for correction, for instruction in righteousness" (1 Tim. 3:16).

2. Who are the two authors of prophecy in the Word of God?

   "No prophecy of Scripture is of private interpretation, for prophecy never came by the will of man, but holy men of God spoke as they were moved by the Holy Spirit" (2 Peter 1:20,21).

3. What helps us understand the Word of God?

   "We have received, not the spirit of the world, but the Spirit who is from God, that we might know the things that have been freely given to us by God" (1Cor. 2:12).

4. What were three things the Christians in Berea did in Bible study?

   "These (from Berea) were more fair-minded . . . in that they received the Word with all readiness, and searched the Scriptures daily to find out whether those things were so" (Acts 17:11).

5. How can we demonstrate we are Christ's disciples?

   "Jesus said to those Jews who believed Him, 'If you abide in My Word, you are My disciples indeed'" (John 8:31).

Bible Study Application

6. How can we abide in Christ's Word?

"He who keeps His commandments abides in Him, and He in him" (1 John 3:24).

7. What should be the first true steps of learning the Bible?

"Blessed is he who reads and those who hear the words of this prophecy, and keep those things written in it" (Rev. 1:3).

8. What is the next step in learning and knowing God?

"Study to show thyself approved of God, a workman that needeth not to be ashamed" (2 Tim. 2:15 KJV).

9. How can we make sure we remember what we learn?

"Your Word I have hidden in my heart, that I might not sin against You" (Psalm 119:11).
"Let the Word of Christ dwell in you richly in all wisdom" (Col. 3:16).

10. How can we make God's Word live in us?

"This book of the law shall not depart from your mouth, but you shall meditate in it day and night, that you may observe to do according to all that is written in it" (Josh. 1:8).

11. What will happen when we take in the Word of God?

"Your words were found and I ate them, and Your Word to me was the joy and rejoicing of my heart" (Jer. 15:16).

Bible Study Application

Checklist

1.	PASSAGE		
2.	POINT	A.	DATE
			PLACE WRITTEN
			PLACE RECEIVED
		B.	SUMMARY OF PASSAGE
		C.	KEY VERSE
		D.	KEY WORDS
		E.	PEOPLE MENTIONED
		F.	WORDS TO LOOK UP IN A DICTIONARY
		G.	PEOPLE, PLACES, AND THINGS TO LOOK UP IN AN ENCYCLOPEDIA
3.	PARALLEL	A.	KEY THOUGHTS IN OTHER REFERENCES
		B.	PARALLEL VERSES WITH SIMILAR MEANING
4.	PROBLEMS	A.	LIST PROBLEMS TO SOLVE FROM THE PASSAGE
		B.	LIST PROBLEMS IN YOUR LIFE THIS PASSAGE SOLVES
5	PRACTICAL	A.	WRITE PRACTICAL PRINCIPLES FROM THE PASSAGE
		B.	WRITE BLESSINGS RECEIVED FROM THE PASSAGE

CHAPTER TWO

STUDYING A BIOGRAPHY

You will want to study the people in the Bible for the difference they made in their time, and the difference they can make in your life. The following people made a significant difference:

- The Woman who Saved a Nation from Genocide (Esther)
- The Dad Whose Drunkenness Influenced His Sons (Noah)
- The Mom Who Imparted Wisdom to Solomon (Bathsheba)
- The Little Girl Who Helped a General Win His Most Challenging Battle (2 Kings 5)
- The Young Boy that Jesus Needed for His Greatest Miracle (John 6).

All these people and hundreds just like them are described in the pages of Scripture waiting to be discovered and taught by teachers.

More than 3,500 individual people are identified in Scripture. Their stories will tell you much about God and about yourself. The teacher who is committed to teaching the Bible cannot avoid teaching biography as part of his or her ministry. But rather than trying to avoid biographies, there are good reasons why teachers may want to use them as often as possible. Teaching biographies can be a highly effective tool to opening up the Bible both for the beginning teacher as well as those more experienced.

Andrew Blackwood, a well-known professor of homiletics, advocated using Bible stories of people. His textbooks have been widely used to train a generation of preachers. In his book *Biographical Preaching for Today*, he states, "A biographical sermon means that the truth of God comes from the Bible passage about a certain character."[1]

Why Study Bible Biographies?

The average American is not interested in dusty history stories but wants to know about people. *People Magazine* is one of the most popular on the newsstand because people are interested in people. Historical fiction and biographical books are consistently among the books most often purchased in bookstores or borrowed from libraries. Most people have little interest in historical trends but are eager to learn about the people who influence history.

When God created people, He intended for them to be social creatures (Gen. 2:18). As a result, people are drawn toward other people. People like people. As a result, biographical lessons are more interesting than other approaches to Bible study. The Psalmist affirmed, "I have rejoiced in the way of Your testimonies (that is, biblical biographies), as much as in all riches (Ps. 119:14).

This social tendency that God gave us means that people not only like people, they identify with people. Your students who struggle to apply a biblical principle to their lives will find it easier when they follow the example of someone else who models that principle. The old adage "monkey see, monkey do" is somewhat derogatory. I like it better this way: "People see, people do." The Psalmist wrote, "I cling to Your testimonies" (Ps. 119:31) and considered them his counselors (Ps. 119:24). Understanding this principle, Paul repeatedly called upon those he reached for Christ to follow the example of the Christian life he modeled for them in his own life (2 Thess. 3:7, 9; 1 Cor. 11:1; Phil. 4:9).

People also gain insights from the life experiences of other people. "The testimony of the LORD is sure, making wise the simple" (Ps. 19:7). God has recorded the lives of various people in Scripture to help us gain His perspective on life. As a result, the student of biblical biographies can claim, "I have more understanding than all my teachers, for Your testimonies are my meditation" (Ps. 119:99). According to Harington Lees, "The lives of men and women who speak to us from the pages of Scripture may be a veritable gold mine of experience to us if we can remember the fact that they lived similar lives and triumphed—by faith, as the writer to the Hebrews reminds us—or, if they entered not into their land of promise, failed through disobedience or unbelief. All good biography is fruitful, but Scripture biography is singularly so."[2]

People learn from people. The ultimate aim of your teaching ministry is that your students learn and apply the important biblical truth you share. Biographies are an effective way to communicate biblical truth to them. Perhaps the Psalmist was thinking of teachers when he wrote, "I will speak of Your testimonies also before kings, and will not be ashamed" (Ps. 119:46). People tend to learn from what they see illustrated in the lives of others as well. The teacher should not be embarrassed to use this effective approach to Bible study regardless of the character or status of Bible study group members.

How to Study a Bible Biography

Find the Life-Message

Everyone has a life-message. What is a life-message? It is simply the contribution—either good or bad—they make because they lived. In approaching biographical study, several steps should be taken to ensure success in gaining a better understanding of the life-message of a particular biblical character. The first step is selecting the character you will study. Usually begin by choosing secondary characters rather than major characters. To begin your study in the life of Peter, Paul, Abraham, or Moses may overwhelm you with biblical material available on the subject's life and times. Herbert Lockyer advises students of biography to "begin with a person whose story is briefly told." He uses the example of Enoch, whose entire life is recorded in six or seven verses of Scripture. There are hundreds of people mentioned in Scripture whose life is summarized in less than a chapter, yet these Bible characters illustrate a significant life-message worth studying.

If you feel you must study a major character, limit your study to a specific aspect of that character's life. Rather than examining the entire life of Moses, why not consider the record of his first forty years in Egypt? If you are studying the life of Joshua, perhaps you should study how Moses mentored Joshua, or Joshua's role during a particular military campaign, such as the battle for Jericho. If your interest in a character continues to grow as you study part of his or her life, you can develop a series on the person. Here are some examples of this approach:

- Faith in the life of Abraham,
- Leadership in the life of Nehemiah, and

- Character development in the life of Peter.

Gather the Data

Once you have decided whom you want to study, begin gathering all available biblical data on the character. Find and read every verse on the person by looking up him or her in an exhaustive concordance. Also, a good topical Bible may describe the person. Don't forget to look in a Bible dictionary or encyclopedia. When a person has more than one name (such as, Abram/Abraham, Jacob/Israel, or Saul/Paul), be certain to check each name. The cross-reference notes in your study Bible will help you gather biblical data that describes your subject.

Look into background and/or ancestry material. Does the Bible identify his or her parents and/or grandparents? How did those parents and/or grandparents shape the character of that child? Is his or her ethnic background clearly identified? How would Esther's background as a Jewish girl in a Persian palace or Ruth's background as a Moabitess in a small Jewish town influence their outlook on life? What about the age in which this person lived? Ahab, Jezebel, Elijah, and Obadiah lived in times of great moral decline in Israel, yet each had his or her unique response to cultural conditions.

As you study the background of your subject, attempt to determine the nature of his or her childhood. A good place to begin is a consideration of the meaning of a child's name. Four hundred years before Christ, Antisthenes said, "The beginning of all instruction is the study of names." The name assigned to a child often reveals the dreams and aspirations parents have for their children. Throughout Scripture, names are used to identify personality traits, occupations, special relationships with God, or some significant symbolic or prophetic reference. Some people live up to their names and fulfill the meaning of their names. Others disappoint their parents. Some even rise above their names and gain a new name by reputation or divine revelation (Simon/Peter, or Saul/Paul).

Lockyer writes, "Truth taught by names is another important aspect to observe. The significance of names opens up a field of pleasant and profitable investigation to all true lovers of Scripture. . . In ancient Israel the name of a person was supposed to indicate some characteristic of that person, or be linked to circumstances, however trivial or monotonous."[3]

Childhood Influences

As you study your character's early childhood and background, consider other hints as to significant early influences in his or her life. What kind of training would a typical child in that era have received? Are there specific references to significant events in that child's early life that give us insight into his or her early character or dreams?

Turning Points

One key to understanding the life-message is tied to significant turning points in someone's life. Look for traumatic events that were likely to influence them. Ask yourself these questions:

- How did the birth of a child or death of a close friend affect your Bible character?
- What would it have been like to live through the famine, battle, or other world crisis that your character experienced?

- What unique encounters with God were turning points in the life of the character you are studying? (For example, Jacob at Penial had his name changed to Israel.)

Character Development

As you begin to formulate a better understanding of your subject, attempt to describe his or her character. Here are some questions that can help you do this.

- What were the conditions when he or she lived? Most of us are influenced by our environment, although many will rise above the conditions of our age.
- Does his or her name suggest a character trait reflected in his or her actions? Did this person live up to his or her name or prove a disappointment to his or her parents who had that dream for their child?
- What kinds of people did this person associate with? You can tell much about a person by the kind of people he or she calls friends.
- Does the Bible ascribe certain characteristics to the person? Check the meaning of the words used with this person to uncover the emphasis intended in describing their morality.
- What kind of influence did this person have on those around him or her? Jesus said, "You will know them by their fruits" (Matt. 7:16).
- Is the evil in this person's life portrayed as an antitype or example to avoid?
- Is there growth or dramatic change in the character of this person in the account of his or her life? Is his or her character redefined in some other part of Scripture?

Major Contributions

As you summarize the life of your subject, compile a list of the major contributions of his or her life.

- Did he or she have a unique office and/or career?
- Was he or she involved in some significant accomplishment?
- Did he or she have a significant influence on someone else who accomplished something special for God and/or his or her society?
- Did some failure in his or her life prevent success in a major undertaking?

Discovering God through Bible Characters

Take time also to identify any insights this person's life might reveal concerning God and His character.

- Could this person be considered a type or antitype of Christ? (Joseph is considered a type of Christ.)
- What do we learn about God in the context of this person's experiences with God?
- Does this person make significant statements concerning God's nature and/or character?

Once Again, the Life-Message

As you conclude your biographical study, identify the single most important principle illustrated in this person's life. What is his or her life-message? Write that principle in a one or two sentences. Then ask yourself four questions to help you understand the principle in the context of your subject's life and its meaning in your life today.

1. How does this principle relate to your personal Christian walk with God?

2. What contemporary life issues are addressed when this principle is applied?

3. What changes do you need to make in your life in light of this biblical principle?

4. How is this principle illustrated in the life of the person being studied?

The strongest biographical lessons you teach will be the ones you first learn as a student of biography.

Once you have completed your personal biographical study, you may wish to consult the research of others. Check your church library for biographical studies of your character or commentaries on the passages which describe that person's life. Those who study and teach biographies on a regular basis will want to add good biographical collections to their personal library. These books will serve as reference tools in the process of developing your biographical studies of biblical characters. At the conclusion of this chapter, you will find a bibliography listing a dozen major biographical collections. While not an exhaustive list, it identifies several books you may wish to add to your personal library.

MAKING THE BIBLE LIVE

1. Observe its facts accurately.
2. Write its meaning correctly.
3. Prize its lesson continually.
4. Apply its principles daily.
5. Obey its commands implicitly.

PRINCIPLES FOR INTERPRETING A BIOGRAPHY

1. Determine the main characteristics or strengths, that is, life-message of the person(s) from the passage of Scripture and the principles by which they lived.
2. Determine the weaknesses, failures, or negative lessons that are found in this person.
3. From other scriptural references, determine what additional information can be found on this person.
4. Determine what influence the family had on them and why.
5. Determine the influence they had on their families or others and why?
6. Determine the conditional promises or threats that apply only to their lives, and the universal promises or threats that apply to your life.
7. Determine the positive principles that could be applied to your life and the negative principles that should be avoided.

How to Teach a Biography

People identify with other people. This explains why you are more likely to attract and maintain interest as you teach biographical lessons than in other kind of Bible study. Still, you must take care to introduce the Bible character in an interesting way.

Case Study

Suggest a case study of a living person. This living person should have a similar life-message to the person being studied. The problem that is addressed in the life of your character will answer the problem raised in the case study.

Hypothetical Situation

A second way to begin might involve asking the question, "What would you do if you found yourself in a situation where . . . ?" Complete that question by describing some contemporary context similar to the experience of the character being studied. Then turn to a biblical character to demonstrate how he or she responded in a similar situation. When a children's worker was called upon to teach a group of children living in foster homes, she told the story of a young boy named "Danny" who was taken from his parents and forced to live in a different culture. Immediately, the children identified with the life of Daniel the Prophet and many were responsive when challenged to "dare to be a Daniel" by determining to serve the Lord rather than conforming to the world.

Problem Solving

A third approach to introducing a biographical study might involve identifying a positive character trait that Christians struggle with in their life. A teacher might ask, "What do you think faith would look like when facing this problem?" The discussion could lead into a study of how Abraham expressed faith in God to solve a variety of problems.

Outline

As you prepare your lesson plan, outline the life of the person being studied. Much of this work has already been done in your personal Bible study, but consider the group you are teaching as you prepare this outline. What approach to this person's life will help them best grasp the principle you are trying to communicate? Sometimes, you will outline the person's life in chronological order. On other occasions, start with a significant event in the person's life and then review the various steps which led up to that event. A third approach might identify an attitude or value and then trace the development of that attitude or value through the various events of that person's life.

The Primary Lesson

Next, identify the primary lesson or lessons to be drawn from this person's life. In each person, his or her life-message. will be reflected in a different way. Is this person a negative example to avoid? Is this person a positive example to imitate? Is there a guiding principle, proverb, or life-message which seems to guide this person's life? Are there steps revealed as the person grows in some area?

Staying on Target

In teaching a biography, it is important to remain focused on the subject of your study. In his book on biographical preaching, Andrew Black-wood warned, "In preaching such a ser-

> ### TEACHING A BIOGRAPHICAL SERIES
>
> *Joseph and His Brothers (Sons of Jacob)*
> *People Who Changed Their World (Judges)*
> *First Ladies (Queens of Israel & Judah)*
> *The Hand that Rocks the Cradle (Mothers)*
> *The Master's Men (The Twelve Disciples)*
> *Paul's Ministry Team (Paul's Companions)*

mon there is a tendency, if not a temptation, to show how much one knows about other men of the Bible."[4] Taking time to draw parallels between your subject and other similar men and women in the Scriptures will cut into the time you have available. If there is a need to consider other similar characters, a better approach would be to teach a series of biographical studies with a focus on a specific character in each study session. The chart on page 44 lists several examples of biographical series you may wish to consider to teach.

Applying the Life-Message

As you look toward the conclusion of this lesson, suggest ways the life-message can be applied in the life of your students. Once again, a series of questions may help you find specific applications of the life-message or principle of someone's life. How would this life-message affect my relationships? How would this life-message change my character and/or personality? How would this life-message help me accomplish a worthy goal? Usually, it is best to focus your application in the specific area most applicable to the members of the group you teach.

When you teach this lesson, help your students become "doers of the word and not hearers only" (James 1:22). Encourage a specific application of a life-message that can be accomplished by your students within the month. Sometimes this will involve identifying a specific action or behavior to copy, for example, to follow the example of Daniel by praying three times daily throughout the week. On other occasions, this will involve addressing a specific attitude, such as, to begin overcoming personal bitterness by asking God to remind you of His sovereign control over your circumstances just as He reminded Joseph of that important truth. A third approach may involve making a significant lifestyle change, for instance, to submit yourself to a Barnabas as did Paul in his early ministry, someone who will hold you accountable in the development of spiritual disciplines and help you experience significant spiritual growth.

Evaluating Your Teaching

If you study and teach biographies often, you will want to periodically take time to evaluate what you have done to stretch yourself to be the best possible student and teacher of the Scriptures. All of us have a tendency to slide into a routine comfort zone which, if unchecked, can cause us to abandon our pursuit of excellence in all we do for God. Blackwood, concerned that preachers of biographical sermons may also become complacent in their work, developed a series of questions he called "The Tests of a Completed Sermon."[5] Blackwood's questions are listed to help you evaluate yourself as you study and teach biographies.

BLACKWOOD'S TESTS OF A BIOGRAPHICAL SERMON

1. *Have I changed the bill of fare often enough?*
2. *Will this sermon interest the men and boys?*
3. *Will my sermon appeal to the intelligence of the hearer, or address him as an inferior?*
4. *Does this message deal fairly with the facts in the Bible passage?*
5. *Throughout this message do I preach mainly in the present tense?*
6. *Does my sermon exalt God the Father, the Son, and the Spirit, or does it move largely on the horizontal level?*

Tools for Biographical Studies

If you study and teach biographies on a regular basis, you may want to invest in a few good biographical collections. These books will serve as reference tools in the process of developing your biographical studies of biblical characters. While not exhaustive, the following list identifies several leading books in this field.

Barnard, David. *Biblical Women.* Cincinnati: Hart & Company, 1863.

Deen, Edith. *All the Women of the Bible.* New York: Harper & Brothers, 1955.

Hastings, James. *The Greater Men and Women of the Bible.* Edinburgh: T. & T. Clark Co.

Kuyper, Abraham. *Women of the Old and New Testaments.* Grand Rapids: Zondervan Publishing House, 1934.

Lockyer, Herbert. *All the Apostles of the Bible.* Grand Rapids: Zondervan Publishing House, 1972.

———. *All the Children of the Bible.* Grand Rapids, Michigan: Zondervan Publishing House, 1986.

———. *All the Kings and Queens of the Bible.* Grand Rapids: Zondervan Publishing House, 1988.

———. *All the Men of the Bible.* Grand Rapids: Zondervan Publishing House, 1958.

———. *All the Women of the Bible.* Grand Rapids: Zondervan Publishing House, 1988.

Towns, Elmer L. *What the Old Testament Is All About: A Study of the History Makers of the Old Testament.* Lynchburg, Va.: Elmer L. Towns, 1995.

———. *What the New Testament Is All About: A Study of the History Makers of the New Testament* (Lynchburg, Va.: Elmer L. Towns, 1995.

Whyte, Alexander. *Bible Characters.* Grand Rapids: Zondervan Publishing House, 1968.

A Biographical Study of Lot
Genesis 11–19

1. Who was Lot?

> "This is the geneology of Terah: Terah beget Abraham, Nahor and Haran. Haran beget Lot" (Gen. 11:27). "Terah took his son Abram and his grandson Lot . . . they went out with them from Ur of the Chaldeans" (Gen. 11:31).

2. What relationship did Lot have to Abram?

> "Now the Lord had said to Abram: get out from your country, from your kindred and from your father's house" (Gen. 12:1). "Lot also, who went with Abram" (Gen. 13:5).

3. What problem caused a separation between the two?

> "There was strife between the herdsmen of Abram's livestock and the herdsmen of Lot's livestock" (Gen. 13:7).

4. How did Abram solve the problem?

> "Abram said to Lot, 'Please let there be no strife . . . please separate from me. If you take the left, then I will go to the right; or if you go to the right, I will go to the left'" (Gen. 13:9).

Bible Study Application

5. On what basis did Lot choose?

> "Lot lifted up his eyes and saw all the plains of Jordan, that it was well watered everywhere . . . like the garden of the Lord" (Gen. 13:10). "Then Lot chose for himself all the plain of Jordan" (Gen. 13:11).

6. What was the first step of Lot's downfall?

> "Lot journeyed east. And they separated from each other" (Gen. 13:11). "Lot dwelt in the cities of the plain and pitched his tent even as far as Sodom" (Gen. 13:12).

7. Read the background of Sodom in a Bible dictionary.

8. Read Genesis 19:1–38 for background.

9. What was Lot's next place?

> "Two angels came to Sodom in the evening, and Lot was sitting in the gate" (Gen. 19:1).

10. What crisis did Lot face?

> "The men of Sodom, both old and young . . . surrounded the house. And they called to Lot . . . 'where are the men (angels) . . .?' Bring them out to us that we may know them carnally" (Gen.19:4, 5).

Bible Study Application

11. How did Lot want to solve the crisis?

> Lot . . . said, "Please my brethren, do not do so wickedly! See now, I have two daughters who have not known a man: please let me bring them out to you, and you may do with them as you wish" (Gen. 13:7, 8).

12. What happened to Lot's wife?

> "They (the angels) said, 'Escape for your life! Do not look behind you nor stay anywhere in the plain'" (Gen. 13:17).

13. What good and bad can be said about Lot?

> "For (if God) delivered righteous Lot, who was oppressed with the filthy conduct of the wicked . . . the Lord knows how to deliver the godly out of temptation" (2 Pet. 2:7, 9).

Bible Study Application

CHECKLIST FOR STUDYING BIOGRAPHIES

1. Who are you studying? (Primary)

   (Other people in passage)

2. Primary reference

   Other references in the Old Testament

   Other references in the New Testament

3. Where was the person?

4. Why was the passage there?

5. What was the person doing? (going?)

6. What was the person thinking and feeling?

7. What problem(s) did the person face?

8. What decision did the person face?

9. How did the person solve the problem(s)?

10. What can you learn about solving problems?

11. What is the greatest quality of this person?

12. What were some supporting qualities in this person?

13. What practical principles can you learn from this person?

CHAPTER THREE

STUDYING A DOCTRINE

Have you ever had someone from a cult come to your front door trying to persuade you to join their movement? Their movements use Christian words, events, and even sing Christian hymns. But they are not Christian when they deny the deity of Christ, that Jesus is the God-Man. These cults have many members who once attended an evangelical church. Whatever else these people may have learned in Christian churches, it is evident they did not learn biblical doctrine. The fact that cults and many other movements like them win converts each year from evangelical churches suggests we are not doing a good job of teaching doctrine.

Biblical doctrine is the foundation of our Christian life and ministry. In the early church, "they continued steadfastly in the apostles' doctrine" (Acts 2:42). One of the marks of spiritual maturity among Christians was "that we should no longer be children, tossed to and fro and carried about with every wind of doctrine, by trickery of men, in the cunning craftiness of deceitful plotting" (Eph. 4:14). Instead, the church was commanded to examine the doctrine taught by various teachers to determine if it was true or not (1 John 4:1; Rev. 2:2). Part of the responsibility of the pastor was to "speak the things which are proper for sound doctrine" (Titus 2:1).

Unfortunately, that has not always been the practice of the evangelical church. A. W. Tozer lamented, "One of the marked differences between the faith of our fathers as conceived by the fathers and the same faith as understood and lived by their children is that the fathers were concerned with the root of the matter, while their present day descendants seem concerned only with fruit."[1]

A more contemporary writer seems to agree with Tozer in his evaluation of the church today when he notes, "Many Christians never leave the first principles of the Gospel. Still spiritual infants, they must be bottle-fed the same formula. When confronted at the door by a representative of another sect, they are helpless to give a reason for the hope that is in them. In the basis of their faith, they are speechless, yet on the reasons for their choice of a house or a car they can discourse at length. This sinful negligence by even one member of the church can cause the whole body to suffer."[2]

Many of your strongest lessons as a teacher will be doctrinal lessons. Doctrinal teaching is the skeleton on which hangs practical Christianity. A body is flabby without the hard bones of a skeleton, so the Christian without a doctrinal foundation is a flabby believer. Philips Brooks commented on the value of doctrinal preaching, applying it to those who would teach a doctrine. According to Brooks, "Preach doctrine, preach all the doctrine that you know, and learn forever more and more, but preach it always, not that men may believe it, but that men may be saved by believing it."[3]

Why Study Bible Doctrine?

There are many reasons why Bible doctrine should be taught in the evangelical church today.

1. *Teaching doctrine is compatible with the purpose of the Scriptures.* "All Scripture is given by inspiration of God, and is profitable for doctrine" (2 Tim. 3:16). You are not teaching the Scriptures as they were intended to be taught if you are not consistently teaching doctrine.

2. *Doctrine is foundational to the Christian life.* Describing the conversion of the Romans, Paul wrote, "But God be thanked that though you were slaves of sin, you obeyed from the heart that form of doctrine to which you were delivered" (Rom. 6:17). It was by "continuing steadfastly in the apostles' doctrine" that the early Christians experienced stability in the Christian life (Acts 2:42).

Paul told Timothy, "Hold fast the pattern of sound words which you have heard from me, in faith and love which are in Christ Jesus" (2 Tim. 1:13). It is the responsibility of teachers to teach sound doctrine, but the purpose of teaching doctrine is not only to teach doctrinal truth. The goal of doctrinal teaching is to help students adopt the Christian lifestyle most appropriate to sound doctrine (Titus 2:1).

When you teach doctrine, you follow the example of our Lord. Jesus, the Master Teacher and our teaching model, was a doctrinal teacher. Jesus told those who followed Him, "My doctrine is not Mine, but His who sent Me. If anyone wills to do His will, he shall know concerning the doctrine, whether it is from God or whether I speak on My own authority" (John 7:16, 17). The people who heard Jesus teach marvelled at His doctrine (Mark 1:27). This was particularly evident when Jesus concluded His Sermon on the Mount: "And so it was, when Jesus had ended these sayings, that the people were astonished at His teaching, for He taught them as one having authority, and not as the scribes" (Matt. 7:28, 29).

Faith and Doctrine

The English word *doctrine* is derived from a Latin term which means "teaching." When you study and teach a doctrine, you are studying and teaching the biblical teaching on some topic or theme. Doctrinal teaching is not an expression of our thoughts on a subject, nor is it an expression of the thoughts of others. Rather, your objective in studying a doctrine is to find out what the Bible teaches about the theme under consideration and to communicate it as accurately as possible. The Scriptures are your source in both the study and teaching of doctrine.

One of the expressions used in the Bible to describe doctrine is "the faith." The Greek word for "faith" can be either a noun or verb. When *faith* is a verb, a person affirms what God has said in His Word (Heb. 11:1). When *faith* is a noun, it is usually preceded with an article *the* and refers to the context of Christianity. "The faith" refers to those things commonly believed by Christians, sometimes called a statement of faith or doctrinal statement. Because doctrinal faith and your personal expression of faith are so closely related, you should not be surprised that the study of doctrine begins with an act of faith. The relationship between faith and doctrine is seen in at least three areas.

First, *only believers have the spiritual insight necessary to understand the things of God.* Paul emphasized this truth in his First Epistle to the Corinthians: "But the natural man [unsaved] does not receive the things of the Spirit of God for they are foolishness to him; nor can he know them, because they are spiritually discerned. But he who is spiritual judges [understands] all things" (1 Cor. 2:14, 15). The Holy Spirit is given to help believers understand the Scripture: "But the Comforter, who is the Holy Spirit, He shall teach you all things" (John 14:26). Believers must exercise faith to allow the Holy Spirit to teach them spiritual truth.

Second, *the student of doctrine must believe in the existence of God, before studying the nature and worth of God.* "But without faith it is impossible to please Him, for he who comes to God must believe that He is, and that He is a rewarder of those who diligently seek Him" (Heb. 11:6). Those who believe in God will be rewarded by God.

In the third place, *the student of doctrine must believe God has revealed Himself to us.* "The secret things belong to the LORD our God, but those things which are revealed belong to us and to our children forever, that we may do all the words of this law" (Deut. 29:29). God has revealed Himself to us through the Old Testament prophets and more fully in the person of Christ described in the New Testament (Heb. 1:1–3).

Growth in the Christian life also involves a growing ability to discern doctrine. Paul rebuked the Corinthians because he "could not speak to you as to spiritual people but as to carnal, as to babes in Christ (1 Cor. 3:1). The Hebrew Christians were also urged to leave "the discussion of the elementary principles of Christ" and go on to greater maturity in Christ (Heb. 6:1–3).

Doctrine and Theology

As you approach the study of doctrine, it is important that you know how it relates to theology. Doctrine is the study of the Bible to learn about God, His work, and His world. Theology involves studying the Bible, plus any and every other source to learn about God and His world. Lewis Sperry Chafer, founding President of Dallas Theological Seminary, defined systematic theology as "the collecting, scientifically arranging, comparing, exhibiting and defending of *all* facts from any and every source concerning God and His works."[4] This definition identifies five steps involved in the study of a topic:

1. *Collecting* data from every source concerning God and His works,

2. *Scientifically arranging* these facts into a logical order,

3. *Comparing and evaluating* our study to determine if they are consistent with the Bible and correspond to reality,

4. *Exhibiting* our conclusions (such as writing them in a doctrinal statement), and

5. *Defending* what we believe from alternative views on that doctrine.

As suggested in this working definition of *theology*, the process of putting together what we believe tends to be somewhat comprehensive, perhaps even too technical for the average believer. Maybe this is why some students of the Bible are

> **BASIC DOCTRINAL STUDIES**
>
> *The Doctrine of the Holy Spirit in Ephesians*
> *The Return of Christ in the Thessalonian Epistles*
> *The Doctrine of the Kingship of Christ in Matthew*

hesitant to study doctrine. They are concerned that doctrinal study might be beyond them and leave them swamped. But, there are ways to overcome this problem and still gain the benefits associated with the study of doctrine. When beginning to study doctrine, it is sometimes best to set limits to avoid becoming bogged down. Study only a small point of one doctrine. This allows you to develop your skills without being swamped with data. The chart on page 58 is an example of doctrinal studies which have been limited in this way.

How to Study a Doctrine

Search the Scriptures

As you approach the study of a doctrine, write a list of all the biblical passages that relate to your topic. You will want to take several steps in compiling this list. First, search a concordance for key words relating to that doctrine. Next, consult a good topical Bible under the heading of the doctrine you are considering. Many study Bibles (reference Bibles) include cross-references designed to lead the reader through a study of biblical topics. This is another good source to use when compiling your list.

Once the list has been compiled, read each passage and make your own brief notes concerning the topic. Remember, the study of a biblical doctrine is built on certain presuppositions. First, your doctrine should be based on the literal interpretation of the Bible. Second, your doctrine should be limited to the Scriptures themselves. Every effort should be made to avoid building doctrine on speculative writings of people or "fancy" ideas that appeal to you imagination.

Arranging the Material

Having completed your study of the biblical data, arrange your basic doctrinal principles in a logical order. In the study of most doctrines, the logical order will become obvious. You will treat it

> ### HOW TO REALLY LEARN THE BIBLE
>
> By copying a Bible passage
> By diagramming sentences.
> By looking up the meaning of words
> By looking for relationships between people
> By reading dictionaries for background
> By finding the meaning of people's names
> By summarizing passages in your own words
> By outlining the passages
> By writing out how you will apply
> By asking for illumination (John 16:13)

with the same importance people in the Bible treat it. Sometimes, it may be helpful to trace doctrinal content in chronological development. Using this approach, Moses' understanding of a certain doctrine becomes foundational to understanding Paul's interpretation of the same doctrine. Occasionally, you may want to highlight and arrange doctrinal emphases by various biblical writers or biblical books. A doctrinal study of the church could be arranged to illustrate the unique emphases of Jesus, Peter, and Paul.

When you arrange your conclusions, take time to look over all the contents. Here is where you harmonize any apparent contradictions. Review key texts where there is an apparent contradiction; never try to make a verse say more than it means. If a conflict remains, there are a couple of principles that will help you resolve it. First, where two verses appear to say different things, the last verse written probably has the fuller revelation of that truth. Give priority to the New Testament over the Old Testament. Second, where one verse appears to say something different than several others, the consistent teaching of many verses is preferred over an interpretation of just one verse. Perhaps, there is something about the context of the odd verse that may explain why it is expressed that way. By checking the context more closely, the problem with the verse often disappears.

No biblical doctrine stands alone. "No Scripture is of private interpretation" (2 Pet. 1:20). If people are created "in the image of God" (Gen. 1:27), what we believe about God is related to what we believe about people. If Christ came to "save His people from their sins" (Matt. 1:21), then our doctrine of Christ is related to our view of salvation and sin. As you review your doctrinal study, consider how your doctrinal conclusions are related to other doctrinal truth taught in the Scriptures. All truth that comes from God is consistent, just as God is a unity (one), He never contradicts Himself. Therefore, our doctrine should be systematic. This means each doctrine should be consistent with others in our doctrinal system.

Outlining the Principles

As you conclude your doctrinal study, read back over your notes. List each principle in an order which best fits the doctrine itself and your approach to studying doctrine. This outline should be helpful in explaining your conclusions to others. Then, identify the biblical text from which you have drawn each principle. If your doctrine is biblical, you should be able to find support for each principle in the Scriptures. Also, others will be able to verify your conclusions by checking the appropriate biblical text.

How to Teach a Doctrine

Some teachers approach the teaching of a doctrine apologetically. This means they begin by defending their beliefs from attacks.

PRINCIPLES FOR INTERPRETING DOCTRINAL PASSAGES

1. Because you want to know God, you begin your doctrinal study to understand the great truths of sin, salvation, and redemption.
2. Because you are a redeemed person, you next study the Scripture to understand the great truths of sin, salvation, and redemption.
3. Your doctrine will come from the meaning of the Bible; you must not try to prove your doctrine with Bible study.
4. Because truth is consistent with itself, you must strive to fit all doctrinal facts into a consistent system.
5. Doctrinal study must always keep practical application in mind.
6. No doctrinal discoveries are "of private interpretation" but will be known by the body of Christ.
7. The general principle taught in all Scripture is preferred over any specific occurrence that seems contradictory

Sometimes it is necessary to build a strong defense, especially when your students are filled with doubts or questions. However, most of the time you will begin like building a house.

You begin with a foundation. Isaiah asked "Whom shall we teach doctrine?" (Isa. 28:29). He answers his question with the process of learning doctrine, "precept upon precept, line upon line" (Isa. 28:10). Teaching doctrine is explaining truth revealed by God in a systematic and understandable way. Teaching that does not include foundational doctrine is teaching without credibility or believability. You must begin where people are and build a foundation on which you can change their lives.

As you begin your doctrinal lesson, begin in a relevant context. Different teachers accomplish this goal in various ways. You may wish to suggest a problem people face or a decision they have difficulty making. Then note the key to making a proper decision is understanding the doctrinal issues surrounding the decision.

Another way to introduce a doctrine is to raise the "Why?" question over common practices in the Christian life and/or society at large. You may wish to ask a question like, "Why do Christians worship on Sunday instead of Saturday," to introduce a lesson on the resurrection of Christ. You may ask, "What percent of your money belongs to God" to introduce a lesson on God's ownership of all things. (The answer is all!) When you begin your session with a "Why?" question, the question should be designed to introduce the doctrinal study as the foundational reason why we express our convictions.

A third way to introduce a doctrinal lesson is to identify a contemporary issue which divides society. At present, issues such as abortion, homosexuality, legalized gambling, and various approaches to education and welfare reform fall into this category. A doctrinal study could be designed to identify biblical principles to help group members determine a Christian perspective on these issues.

As you prepare to present your doctrinal lesson, consider your students and remember the principle of progressive revelation. Progressive revelation describes the process of how God revealed truth over sixteen hundred years. The Old Testament foundation was established slowly before the more complete revelation of God was revealed in Christ: "Long ago God spoke many times and in many ways . . . now in these final days He has spoken to us through His Son" (Heb. 1:1, 2 NLT). How does this principle of progressive revelation relate to your class? First, if many of your students are unsaved or only new Christians, they need to know that God gave people everything they needed to know, and everyone had enough information about God to be saved. Second, they need to know that Christ is the final revelation of God, and in Him there is all we can know of God. Regardless of the maturity level of those you teach, there is rarely any value in dealing with speculative ideas. Therefore, minimize time spent in these areas.

Take time to consider the best way to present your doctrinal summary. Usually this will involve one of three approaches. One approach defines the doctrinal *words* and explains the implications of your statement. A good working definition of a doctrine will suggest its own teaching

FULL MENTION CHAPTERS

Love . . . .*I Corinthians 13*
Faith . . . .*Hebrews 11*
Resurrection . . . .*I Corinthians 15*
The Lord's Table . . . .*I Corinthians 11*
The Old Nature. . . . . *Romans 7*
The Holy Spirit . . . . *Romans 8*
The Millennium. . . . . . *Revelation 20*
The Rapture. . . . . . .*I Thessalonians 4*

outline. A second approach is to begin with the *first mention* of a doctrine in Scripture. You begin your lesson where the Bible first introduces a topic. This is usually an embryonic statement that will have fuller explanation at another place in Scripture. Using this approach, other verses are consulted to draw out the fuller meaning of the text. In a third approach, you explain a doctrine in the context of its *full mention* in Scripture. There is usually a chapter or book which emphasizes that doctrine. When using this approach, the doctrinal lesson may not be much different from a chapter or book study described in a later chapter in this book.

Take care to present a strong case for your doctrine. Several guidelines will help you as you prepare your presentation. First, be careful not to weaken strong Scripture texts by using weak texts that stretch a point. Second, be certain to define technical terms clearly and accurately. It's all right to use doctrinal terms; just make sure people understand them. Do not spend too much time trying to explain away "hard" verses. Also, avoid the trap of making a minor doctrine the key to all others. Finally, place your doctrinal lesson in the larger context of the important issues of Christianity—issues like salvation, knowing God, serving God, and loving others.

Biblical doctrine should make a difference in your life. Therefore, when you teach a doctrine, suggest ways your doctrine can be applied to the lives of your students. A believing doctrine is a behaving doctrine. The logical application of a biblical doctrine can usually be uncovered quickly by asking a couple of key questions. First, "How is this doctrine most likely to be expressed in the Christian life?" Second, "What changes need to be made to bring my life in line with the teachings of this doctrine?"

As you ask yourself these questions, consider a special project that would help you and your group apply the doctrine. Encourage a specific application of the doctrine which can be accomplished by your students within thirty days. If you are teaching a lesson on the doctrine of revelation, consider challenging your students to begin reading a chapter of the Bible each day for the next month. After studying the doctrine of the Holy Spirit, ask your students to yield themselves to be filled with the Holy Spirit. In response to a study on the attributes of God, ask your students to begin each day by singing a hymn or praise chorus to worship God by recognizing one of His attributes.

God inspired the Scriptures making them "profitable for doctrine." As we study and teach the Bible doctrinally, we can do so with the assurance we are studying and teaching the Bible in a manner consistent with God's purpose.

Tools for Doctrinal Studies

If you study and teach doctrine on a regular basis, you may want to invest in a few good theology books. These books will serve as reference tools in the process of developing and evaluating your doctrinal studies. While not exhaustive, the following list identifies several leading books in this field.

Chafer, Lewis Sperry. *Systematic Theology.* 2 vols. Wheaton, Ill.: Victor Books, 1988.

Elwell, Walter A. *Evangelical Dictionary of Biblical Theology.* Grand Rapids: Baker Book House, 1996.

Erickson, Millard J. *Christian Theology.* Grand Rapids: Baker Book House, 1986.

Lockyer, Herbert. *All the Doctrines of the Bible.* Grand Rapids: Zondervan Publishing House, 1988.

Ryrie, Charles C. *Basic Theology.* Wheaton, Ill.: Victor Books, 1986.

Thiessen, Henry Clarence. *Lectures in Systematic Theology.* Grand Rapids: Wm. B. Eerdmans Publishing Company, 1951.

Towns, Elmer L. *Theology for Today.* Lynchburg, Va.: Elmer L. Towns, 1994. A systematic theology for college and seminary students.

————. *What the Faith is All About.* Wheaton: Tyndale House Publishers, 1983. A Bible doctrine book for lay people.

A Doctrinal Study of the Church Acts 2:41-47

1. *Who grows the church? (notice 2 personal pronouns).*

"The Lord added to the church daily those who were being saved" (Acts 2:47).

2. *What does God use to grow the church?*

"I (Jesus) will build my church, and the gates of Hades shall not prevail against it" (Matt. 18:18). "The Lord added to the church daily those who were being saved" (Acts 2:47).

3. *What meaning does this new term give to the church?*

"Gave Him (Christ) to be hear over all things to the church, which is His body" (Eph. 1:22, 23).

4. *What 2 things happened to those who were added to the church?*

"Those that gladly received His word were baptized; and that day about three thousand souls were added to them" (Acts 2:41).

5. *What 4 things did believers first do?*

"They continued steadfastly in the apostles' doctrine and fellowship, in the breaking of bread and in prayers" (Acts 2:42).

Bible Study Application

6. List the words and numbers that describe church growth?

"In the midst of the disciples (altogether the number of names was about a hundred and twenty" (Acts 1:15). "Three thousand souls were added" (2:41). "The number of the men came to be about five thousand" (4:4). "The disciples multiplied greatly in Jerusalem" (6:7).

7. What were two ministries of a growing church?

"Daily in the temple, and in every house, they did not cease teaching and preaching Jesus as the Christ" (Acts 5:42).

8. What two influences did a growing church have on the community?

"Then fear came upon every soul, and many signs and wonders were done through the apostles" (Acts 2:43). "Having favor with all the people" (Acts 2:47).

9. What is the three-fold work of church leaders?

"He Himself gave some to be apostles, some prophets, some evangelists, and some pastors and teachers, for the equipping of the saints, for the work of ministry, for the edifying of the body of Christ" (Eph. 4:11,12).

10. How can believers build the church?

"For from you (the church at Thessalonica) the word of the Lord has sounded forth, not only in Macedonia and Achaia, but also in every place your faith toward God has gone out" (1 Thess. 1:8).

Bible Study Application

A CHECKLIST FOR STUDYING DOCTRINE

1. What doctrine are you studying?

2. What is the primary passage(s)?

   (What does it teach about the doctrine?)
   (Supporting OT passages)

   (What do they teach about the doctrine?)
   (Supporting NT passages)

   (What do they teach about the doctrine?)

3. What biblical person is associated with this doctrine? (OT)

4. How did the doctrine influence their life?

5. Summarize the doctrine.

6. What principles are taught in this doctrine?

7. How will you practically apply this doctrine?

8. What happens when this doctrine is ignored or denied?

9. How deep is your commitment to this doctrine?

CHAPTER FOUR

STUDYING THE BIBLE DEVOTIONALLY

One of the great dangers in personal Bible study is that these important doctrines become ends in themselves. The same can happen with teaching the Bible. We let the Word of God become the aim of teaching, rather than making our aim the building up of people and making them mature in Christ. We must study the Bible for the greater purpose of learning how to live. Paul reminded Timothy of this goal: "All Scripture is given by inspiration of God, and is profitable for doctrine, for reproof, for correction, for instruction in righteousness, that the man of God may be complete, thoroughly equipped for every good work" (2 Tim. 3:16, 17).

There are many approaches to studying and teaching the Bible in this book. Each chapter is designed to help you grow in Christ. But this chapter is more compelling because it moves us beyond learning the contents of Scripture to personal application of the principles and spirit of the Scriptures. This chapter wants to help you become more spiritual, and the devotional approach to Bible study and teaching has great value for this purpose. After discussing nine different approaches to the study the Book of Galatians, Merrill C. Tenney concludes that the devotional approach is the crown of Bible study:

> These methods may produce a good understanding of the letter of the epistle; but a mere knowledge of its facts and style will never impress its real message upon a believing heart. The crown of all study is the devotional method, by which the truths ascertained through the various means already described are integrated and applied to the needs of the individual.[1]

This same high view of the devotional approach to Bible study was also held by Howard Vos. In his survey of sixteen different approaches to Bible study, he noted that the devotional approach makes us spiritual:

> The end in view in all devotional Bible study is the improvement of the individual's spiritual life by discovering in the Word the claims of God upon the believer and His instructions for living and enhancing the Christian life ... The devotional method may be effectively executed by means of a careful study of words, verses, paragraphs, chapters, books, Biblical characters, and Christ in a given portion.[2]

You will use a variety of approaches to study and teach the Bible, but especially you will be concerned with life application. As you use the various methods of Bible study and teaching to communicate biblical content, you will lay a foundation in the life of your students. When you have laid that foundation, the devotional approach to the Bible will help you guide students to apply their biblical knowledge to life. When this is done, the Holy Spirit, who is your Teacher, will use the Scripture to effectively change students' lives. That is the ultimate goal of Bible teaching ministry.

Why Study the Bible Devotionally?

1. *Studying the Bible devotionally will help you love the Lord.* Jesus spoke of "the great commandment." When challenged by a Pharisee just a few days before His death to identify "the great commandment in the law" (Matt. 22:36), Jesus responded, "You shall love the LORD your God with all your heart, with all your soul, and with all your mind. This is the first and great commandment" (Matt. 22:37, 38). A devotional understanding of the Scriptures helps us love God more and more as we grow in Him.

2. *Studying the Bible devotionally will help you overcome sin.* The Psalmist wrote, "How can a young man cleanse his way? By taking heed according to Your word. With my whole heart I have sought You; Oh, let me not wander from Your commandments! Your word I have hidden in my heart, that I might not sin against You" (Ps. 119:9–11). The person was right who wrote in the flyleaf of the Bible of evangelist Dwight L. Moody, "This book will keep you from sin, or sin will keep you from this book." Studying the Bible devotionally will help us achieve victory over sin in our lives.

3. *Reading the Bible devotionally will help you meditate.* Meditating on the Scripture is one of the biblical keys to success in life. God told Joshua, "This Book of the Law shall not depart from your mouth, but you shall meditate in it day and night, that you may observe to do according to all that is written in it. For

then you will make your way prosperous, and then you will have good success" (Josh. 1:8). Also, meditating on the Scriptures is one of the keys to personal fulfillment in life. The "blessed man" is described in the first psalm: "But his delight is in the law of the LORD, and in His law he meditates day and night" (Ps. 1:2).

4. *Reading the Bible devotionally will bring significant change to your life.* More than other approaches to the Scriptures, this approach relates directly to the practical expression of our faith in living for Christ. Therefore, this approach will help us accomplish the work we are most committed to doing.

How to Study the Bible Devotionally

Before we can consistently *teach* the Bible to change the lives of our students, we must first learn to *study* the Bible devotionally. Unlike other approaches to Bible study, the key to studying the Bible devotionally is not so much in methodology as in attitude. This is what Merrill C. Tenney says about the spirit of devotional study:

> Devotional study is not so much a technique as a spirit. It is the spirit of eagerness which seeks the mind of God; it is the spirit of humility which listens readily to the voice of God; it is the spirit of adventure which pursues earnestly the will of God; it is the spirit of adoration which rests in the presence of God.[3]

Here are some suggestions to help you read the Bible devotionally:

1. *Begin your Bible study time with prayer.* As you pray, focus upon who God is and express your appreciation to Him for re-

vealing truth to His people (Deut. 29:29). Many teachers find it helpful to pray a prayer similar to that of the Psalmist as he approached the Scriptures: "Open my eyes, that I may see wondrous things from Your law" (Ps. 119:18).

2. *Take time to choose a passage that lends itself to devotional reading.* While all Scripture tells us about God, certain parts of Scripture tend to be better suited to devotional study than others. The Psalms lend themselves to this approach because they were written passionately for God. The Psalmist is concerned about knowing God experimentally, and your students can seek God with that same passion. Also, extended passages such as the Sermon on the Mount (Matt. 5–7) or the Upper Room Discourse (John 13–18) lend themselves to application. Normally, you will study shorter passages when approaching the Bible devotionally.

3. *Give yourself time.* One pastor commented he took an extended time Monday to study and apply devotionally the passage he would preach next Sunday. He said it was more important to feel the Lord speak to him through the passage before he prepared a sermon to speak to others.

4. *Read the passage several times.* You may want to emphasize different verses and/or words during each reading. Also, you may wish to commit parts of the passage to memory so you can meditate on them. When you commit the Scriptures to memory, you can meditate on them even outside of your study time. According to Deuteronomy 6:7, the four best times of the day to meditate on Scriptures you have memorized are:

- When you find yourself sitting and waiting,

- When you commute from place to place,
- When you go to bed each evening, and
- When you wake up each morning.

5. *Give some attention to your method of devotional Bible reading.* Ask yourself these basic questions to discover the message of the passage:

> **8 STEPS TO APPLICATION**
>
> *Truths to Believe*
> *Actions to Imitate*
> *Attitudes to Desire*
> *Sins to Confess*
> *Habits to Forsake*
> *Examples to Follow*
> *Promises to Claim*
> *Commands to Obey*

- What is the primary emphasis or subject in this passage?
- Who is (are) the key character(s) in this passage?
- Is there any significance in the meaning of his or her name?
- What is the key verse in the passage I am studying?

6. *Look for special insights in the passage relating to your relationship with Christ.* What does this passage teach that God does for you? What should you do for God? What practical principles are intended in this chapter? Apply these principles to daily living. How do they make you feel? Do you love God more? Do you want to worship Him more? What energy do you get from the passage?

7. *Give special consideration to the key verse of the passage.* Key verses jump out at us and make us remember what is taught in a passage. They are important for two reasons: first, because they summarize the heart of the message; and second, because they are pivotal in the development of the context of the passage.

8. *Consider the meaning of key words in the passage.* Begin by compiling a list of words which are used several times or words which are significant to the passage. Then look for answers to several questions about these words. How is this word used in other places in Scriptures? Does this writer tend to use this word in a unique way? What did this word mean to those who first read it? Does this word reveal some significant truth about God, people, sin, or salvation? How can this word be applied to strengthen one's personal walk with God? Finding the answers to these and similar questions will help you better understand and appreciate the message of the passage.

9. *Look for things in the passage that address special concerns in the Christian life.* Once again, several questions can guide you in this aspect of your study:

   • Is there an example to follow?
   • Is there an error to avoid?
   • Is there a responsibility to fulfill?
   • Is there a promise to claim?
   • Is there a prayer to pray?

As you list the answers to these questions, you are identifying specific applications which can be made to life.

10. *Use discernment in applying the Scriptures devotionally to your life.* If you have not been careful in your study of the Scriptures, you may find yourself attempting to apply something which violates a biblical principle or may not be the teaching of that passage. First, distinguish between what the Bible *describes* and what it *dictates*. David's marriage to eight wives is descriptive. You should not follow his practice; the

WHEN TO CLAIM BIBLE PROMISES

It is not necessarily true that, "Every promise in the Book is mine, every chapter, every verse, every line." While all Scripture has principles to guide our lives, we cannot claim every promise, because some promises do not apply to us. When can we claim a Bible promise?

1. *A Bible promise is for you if it is universal in scope. You can claim, "Whosoever believeth in Him shall not perish."*
2. *It is not for you if it was personal to someone else. You cannot claim, "Be not afraid, but speak . . . no man shall set upon thee to hurt thee" (Acts 18:9,10).*
3. *It is for you if it is for all time. You can claim, "In all thy ways acknowledge Him, and He will direct thy paths" (Prov. 3:6).*
4. *It is not you if it was conditional to a person(s). You cannot claim as could the land of Israel, "Every place that the sole of your foot shall tread upon, that have I given you" (Joshua 1:3).*
5. *It is for you if it is conditional for all. You can claim, "Draw nigh unto God, and He will draw nigh to you" (James 4:8).*
6. *It is not for you if it violates the literal interpretation of Scripture. We wrongly think the main reason God doesn't answer your prayers is, "Ye have not because ye ask not" (James 4:2).*
7. *It is for you if you know God's principle that is taught in the passage and you apply it to your time and culture.*

Bible describes both the positive examples and negative deeds of God's people. The Scriptures dictate monogamy rather than polygamy as the pattern for a healthy marriage. Next, specific commands to individuals do not necessarily apply to everyone. Jesus' command to "tarry in Jerusalem" does not mean every Christian should go to the Holy Land to seek God's power and the filling of the Holy Spirit. Third, distinguish between cultural expressions and eternal principles. The Nazarite vow is a cultural expression. The Nazarite vow was made under the law in the Old Testament for certain purposes. The eternal principle is for people to make an outward commitment to God when they want to make an inward decision to follow Him. Men who want to be more committed to God today do not need to grow beards or long hair, as did the Nazarites. Further, be sure of the meaning of the context of and conditions associated with a promise before claiming it in your life. Is the promise universal or limited in scope? Is the promise personal or applicable to all? Is the promise conditional or unconditional? Is the promise for us or for people of another time?

Some Christians use a devotional approach to Bible study as an excuse to find deeper truths and hidden meanings in a passage. Someone once said of a devotional preacher, "He can find hidden things in the Bible that God never put there." As you look for deeper truths and hidden meanings in a passage, you should exercise caution. That does not mean there are no deeper truths to explore. On the contrary, sometimes the meaning of names sheds light on the character of people. There may also be significance attached to the use of certain numbers in the Bible. Throughout the Scriptures, various types are suggested in people and events which illustrate truths concerning Christ, the church, and/or the Christian life. Also, some things mentioned in Scripture are described as symbols or mysteries of some other, deeper truth. The safe approach in these areas is to let the Scriptures interpret themselves in the light of other Scriptures.

How to Teach the Bible Devotionally

Just as attitude is important in studying the Bible devotionally, so our attitude is imperative when teaching the Bible devotionally. Our goal is to lead students deeper in their love for God and their commitment to Him. The old farmer said his Christianity was better

PRINCIPLES FOR INTERPRETING DEVOTIONAL STUDY

1. Every passage will have one interpretation governed by literal interpretation, but will also have many applications.
2. Be careful of "spiritualizing" the Bible to make it say something apart from the meaning of the text.
3. The Bible is a book of principles to guide our daily lives and service.
4. Know the difference between **descriptions** of situations that do not apply today and **prescriptions** that were written to guide our lives.
5. Apply to your life those direct applications where the Bible generally censors or approves all.
6. Explicit commands to individuals are not always the will of God for you today.
7. Apply to your life the obvious principles in the lives of people in Scripture.
8. You do not need to be in the exact situation that involved a person in the Bible, to apply their principles to your lives.

"felt" than "telt." Teachers who will be effective in the devotional approach to Bible teaching will find value in being transparent with others. They must share their devotional life with their students.

In using this approach, begin with a commitment to teach the Bible devotionally, rather than trying to cram the Bible into a devotional thought.

- Avoid taking a phrase from the Bible because of its wording and using it in a different sense than it was intended.

- Avoid imposing a meaning on the Scriptures that was never intended.

- Avoid treating the Scriptures as an allegory (like a fairy tale) and emphasizing a speculated message over the clear teaching of Scripture.

Get Their Interest

How you introduce a devotional Bible study will either stimulate interest or discourage further investigation. Therefore, begin a devotional lesson by talking about something relevant to their Christian lives. Raise issues of worship before studying a worship Psalm. Raise the issue of the students' relationship to others before the study of a passage that discusses our relationship with God and others.

Usually, you begin your study by outlining a passage, so begin your teaching by doing the same thing. Then show your pupils the context of the passage. Next, focus on a key character in the passage. Point out to your students the key verse in this passage. Tell them why the verse is a key verse and what it means to your life. Next, point out the significant words in this passage. Have them find the words and circle them in their Bibles.

Apply the Message

As you teach this lesson, lead your students to discover special applications that are relevant to the Christian life.

- Help them find the answers to important questions.
- Point out examples to follow.
- Point out a responsibility to fulfill.
- Point out a promise to claim.
- Focus on a prayer to pray.

Then pray it with them.

As you continue to guide students in their study, discuss ways the students can apply the principles to their lives. Ask which principle they would rate as most important in their life right now. Then ask them how this principle would improve the quality of their Christian life. Guide them to identify and state the steps they could take to implement this principle this week. Once those steps have been identified, you must challenge them to begin taking those steps this week.

Closing the Lesson

Conclude your devotional lesson by expressing your devotion to God. There are several ways to do this. You may want to share a testimony of what God has done in your life. You may make a public vow or promise that grows out of the lesson. You may want to close the lesson in quiet meditation. On another occasion, you may choose to express your commitment to pray privately or quietly, or in a hymn or praise chorus. You may be more comfortable praying together with others about the things they are planning to implement in their lives. A wise teacher will vary these approaches periodically as he or she teaches the Bible devotionally.

Sometimes teachers teach the Bible devotionally by modeling their own devotional study. One college Bible teacher, concerned his students were beginning to treat the Bible as just another textbook, helped a class to work through a passage of Scripture. The teacher helped students uncover life-changing truths from the Scriptures for themselves.

On another occasion, a pastor knew several seminary students were having difficulty with maintaining a personal time alone with God each day. When the pastor spoke in seminary chapel, he explained how his personal devotions for that day related to his chapel message of that day. He showed the students how to do their own personal devotions, and this encouraged them to do the same thing in their own lives. Both Jesus and Paul used this approach to teach others some important principles of the Christian life.

Tools for Devotional Studies

Those teachers committed to studying and teaching the Bible devotionally on a regular basis may want to develop a good library to assist them in their study. These books will serve as reference tools in the process of developing and evaluating your own devotional studies. There are many authors and publishers of devotional commentaries and books on the Christian life. While not exhaustive, the following list identifies several leading books in this field.

Our Daily Bread. Grand Rapids: Radio Bible Class.

Chambers, Oswald. *My Utmost for His Highest.* New York: Dodd, Mead & Company, 1934.

Henry, Matthew. *Commentary on the Whole Bible.* Grand Rapids: Zondervan Publishing House, 1980.

Ironside, H. A. *In the Heavenlies.* Neptune, N.J.: Loizeaux Brothers. Ironside wrote devotional commentaries on many biblical books although his commentary on the Epistle to the Ephesians may be the best known.

Murray, Andrew. *Absolute Surrender.* Murray wrote many other books on the Christian life which the teacher using the devotional method might find helpful.

Spurgeon, Charles Haddon. *The Treasury of David.* Nashville: Thomas Nelson Publishers.

Towns, Elmer L. *Understanding the Deeper Life: A Guide to Christian Experience.* Old Tappan, N.J.: Fleming H. Revell Company, 1988.

Tozer, A. W. *The Knowledge of the Holy.* New York: Harper & Brothers, 1961.

Vine, W. E. *Expository Dictionary of Old and New Testament Words.* Old Tappan, N.J.: Fleming H. Revell Company.

A Devotional Bible Study on Worship Psalm 100

1. What people, beyond believers, does God want to worship Him?

> *"Make a joyful shout to the LORD, all you lands" (Ps. 100:1).*

2. When will the unsaved join believers in worshiping Him?

> *"Therefore, God hath highly exalted Him and given Him the name which is above every name, that at the name of Jesus every knee should bow in heaven, and of those on earth, and those under the earth, and that every tongue should confess that Jesus Christ is Lord" (Phil. 2:9–11).*

3. Why are we commanded to "shout to the Lord"?

> *"True worshipers will worship the Lord in spirit and truth, for the Father seeketh such to worship Him" (John 4:23).*

4. What are three ways we can worship God?

> *"Serve the LORD with gladness; come before His presence with singing. Know that the LORD, He is God" (Ps. 100:2, 3).*

5. What four things we can know that will motivate us to worship the Lord?

> *"Know . . . it is He who has made us, and not we ourselves; We are His people, and the sheep of His pasture" (Ps. 100:3).*

6. How can you worship God your Creator for creating you?

> *"Know . . . it is He who has made us, and not we ourselves" (Ps. 100:3).*

Bible Study Application

7. How can you worship God your Protector for caring for you?

> "We are his people, and the sheep of His pasture (Ps. 100:3).

8. What 2 responses should begin your worship?

> "Enter into his presence with thanksgiving, and into His courts with praise" (Ps. 100:4).

9. The Psalmist repeats these 2 responses. How will you use them?

> "Be thankful to Him, and bless His holy name" (Ps. 100:3).

10. What 3 attributes of God does the Psalmist include in his benediction?

> "For the LORD is good; His mercy is everlasting, and His truth endures to all generations" (Ps. 100:5).

Thank God for being good to you.

How has God's mercy blessed you?

How are you grateful for His truth?

11. Can you list His other suggested names beyond the two listed? "Know that the LORD, He is God" (v. 3).

If we are sheep, He is _____ .
If we enter His courts, He is _____ .
If we serve him, He is _____ .
If we are created, _____ .
Other names of God _____ .

Bible Study Application

A Checklist for Devotional Bible Studies

1. What did you read today? (reference)
   _____

2. Where did you read today? (place)
   _____

3. What is your greatest need today?
   _____

4. What promise did you find? (reference)
   (Is it a universal promise?)
   _____

   (What are the conditions?)
   _____

   (How will you claim it?)
   _____

5. What command did you find? (reference)
   _____

   (How will you obey it?)
   _____

6. What is God's message for today?
   _____

7. How will you apply it?
   _____

CHAPTER FIVE

STUDYING PARABLES

A traveller who is beaten and robbed by thieves but helped by a stranger. A farmer casting seed in rocky soil. A woman misplacing a coin and later finding it. A sheep that wanders off into danger but is later found by the shepherd. At different times, Jesus used each of these common stories to teach people truths about God and His work in our lives. The stories He built around these everyday things in life are called parables.

One day, an expert in Jewish law challenged Jesus with the question, "Teacher, what shall I do to inherit eternal life?" (Luke 10:25). Knowing He was being set up, Jesus asked the expert a question of his own, "What is written in the law? What is your reading of it?" (Luke 10:26). The man responded with a widely accepted summary statement of the law: " 'You shall love the LORD your God with all your heart, with all your soul, and with all your strength, and with all your mind,' and your neighbor as yourself" (Luke 10:27). Both

Jesus and His challenger found agreement in the statement, but to each it meant something different. Jesus knew the law was written to show us how far short we fall of God's standard of righteousness. The challenger viewed the law as a tool to demonstrate just how righteous he was. One more question was all it took to demonstrate just how far apart these two views were. Jesus asked, "And who is my neighbor?" (Luke 10:29).

In response to that question, Jesus told what has become His best-known parable, that of the Good Samaritan. It is the story of a traveller who is robbed, beaten, and left to die. Two religious leaders who might be expected to help him saw the man in need but passed on by. In contrast, a Samaritan, a member of a race which normally had nothing to do with the Jews, saw the man in need but took time to care for him. When the Samaritan had to move on before the man was completely recovered, he paid someone else to continue caring for the man who had been left to die. Jesus never answered the challenger's question, but by the end of the story the answer was evident to everyone listening.

Jesus used parables throughout His teaching ministry to communicate significant truths in a simple way. "All these things Jesus spoke to the multitude in parables; and without a parable He did not speak to them, that it might be fulfilled which was spoken by the prophet, saying: 'I will open My mouth in parables; I will utter things kept secret from the foundation of the world'" (Matt. 13:34, 35).

What is a Parable?

At its very core, a parable is simply a story. It is a dramatic recording of actions that lead to a conclusion. It describes characters who interact with one another or have significant things to say. The parables of Jesus are true to life, but they are not narratives of actual events. They were not myths about flying horses or talking objects in nature. Neither are they necessarily based on specific historical events. The story may not have actually happened as told, but the story was realistic enough. It may well have happened just as it was described. While storytelling has been a form of entertainment for generations, the primary focus of biblical parables is the teaching of some spiritual truth. These truths are drawn from the similarities between events in the story and life in general. Parables are one of the means God has chosen to reveal Himself and His truth to us in both the Old and New Testaments.

Someone has described a miracle as the truth of God in works. In a different sense, a parable may be described as the truth of God in words. While Jesus often used miracles to draw attention to some specific principle He was trying to teach, when using parables He chose not to include any miraculous acts. Also, just as miracles were effective in drawing large crowds to Jesus, so the people gathered to hear Jesus teach in parables. Parables became one of His most popular forms of teaching.

In parables, the infinite and unlimited God condescended to convey infinite truth to finite and limited people in a very finite and limited way. These parables included familiar events, places, things, and different types of people. This teaching tool may well have been the best available tool that Jesus used in his teaching methods. Despite their effectiveness in both the Old Testament and during the ministry of Jesus, extended parables were not widely used after the death of Christ. Perhaps the parables of Jesus set such a high standard that other teachers in the ages since have been reluctant to place their own stories alongside His.

The word *parable* is derived from the Greek word *parabole*, which is a compound of two other words. The Greek preposition *para* means "beside." The Greek verb *ballein* means "to cast or throw down." The word *parable* literally means to place one thing by the side of another.

These stories were designed to encourage the application of truth from parallel observation. Those who heard Jesus teach in

> **An Earthly Story with a Heavenly Meaning**

parables were motivated to learn more. They came to Jesus and asked, "Explain this parable to us" (Matt. 15:15). Jesus used parables to apply important spiritual truth to life. He taught His disciples, "Now learn this parable from the fig tree . . ." (Matt. 24:32). After making His point in the Parable of the Good Samaritan, Jesus challenged His would-be challenger, "Go and do likewise" (Luke 10:37).

Many have attempted to define parables in a popular manner that is easier for people to remember. They have been called "an outward symbol of an inward reality." A more technical description suggests a parable is "a figure that teaches spiritual truth by contrast or similarity." Perhaps the definition most people find easiest to remember is that which encourages us to think of a parable as "an earthly story with a heavenly meaning."

Why Study the Parables?

Jesus, the Master Teacher, used parables widely and effectively in His teaching ministry. That fact alone should motivate us to use this method to teach our stories and to teach the stories of Jesus. Even if Jesus had not effectively used parables in His ministry, there would still be valid reasons why we should teach the parables. Many of these reasons may have motivated Jesus Himself in choosing these effective methods.

1. *We should study the parables because of their enduring quality.* Cultures and times have changed significantly in the past twenty centuries, yet these stories Jesus told in first-century Israel continue to be relevant in American towns and cities today. These stories transcend cultures because they are about people. While the trappings of our culture change from generation to generation, people remain essentially the same.

2. *We should study the parables because they are easy to remember.* People tend to remember stories better than abstract ideas or propositional truth. This is why pastors use illustrations in their sermons. While ministers are primarily concerned with teaching a biblical principle, they understand this is often best communicated when illustrated with stories. When Jesus was asked, "Why do You speak to them in parables?" (Matt. 13:10), Jesus gave an application and concluded with the words, "Therefore I speak to them in parables" (Matt. 13:13). The word "therefore" implies Jesus' plain language had been ineffective in communicating truth to the people. Parables helped Him overcome this problem.

3. *We should study the parables because they motivate us to learn.* People like to learn when teachers make learning interesting to people. Jesus used parables to make new truth interesting to His hearers. In doing so, He applied a principle that is widely applied today in the entertainment industry. People will read a novel, listen to a song, or watch a movie or video because

they are interesting, but in the process they will also learn information and adopt the values that the author communicates through that media. George Bernard Shaw once boasted he could teach people anything so long as he kept them laughing. By this he meant that he could communicate values people would normally reject and they would accept them if his stories maintained a high quality of entertainment.

4. *We should study the parables because they keep our attention.* There were times when people would interrupt Jesus in the midst of a sermon if they disagreed with his conclusions. The apostles often found themselves "disputing" in the synagogues as they attempted to explain the gospel to those gathered. But there is no recorded instance of anyone interrupting a parable. A good story told by a good storyteller will both arrest and hold the attention of the hearers. Jesus told the best stories in His parables, and He taught them well.

5. *We should study the parables because they help people gain and remember significant truth.* These stories force people to think through the principle. In doing so, the principle becomes a part of who they are. The adventure of discovery is part of the learning process itself. People never forget what they think out themselves. When Jesus told parables, He used a teaching method that ensured the lesson would be remembered longer.

6. *We should study the parables because they hide truth from those who are resistant.* Jesus was asked, "Why do You speak to them in parables?" (Matt. 13:10). One reason was to conceal truth from the disinterested or those in rebellion against Him: "Because it has been given to you to know the mysteries of the

kingdom of heaven, but to them it has not been given" (Matt. 13:11). Jesus used parables to teach the teachable and hide truth from those who hardened their hearts to His message.

Interpreting the Parables

Throughout the centuries, students of parables have taken great liberty in interpreting the "hidden meanings" in these simple stories. In the fifth century, Augustine was doing no more than his contemporaries when he "discovered" deep theological truth in the Parable of the Good Samaritan. As the man went "down from Jerusalem, he became a vivid picture of Adam leaving the presence of God in the garden. Jericho became the city of mortality. The devil himself became part of the drama as thieves appeared on the scene. The beating the man received was a picture of Adam being persuaded to sin. The failure of a priest and Levite to assist demonstrated the inability of the Old Testament to assist man in his sinful state. The binding of wounds marked the restraint of sin. The oil was a symbol of good hope. Wine represented a fervent spirit. The beast upon which the injured man was laid was the flesh of Christ. The inn became the church. The next day was said to refer to a time "after the resurrection." While much Augustine had to say may have been doctrinally sound and edifying to those who heard him preach, it is doubtful if Jesus had all that in mind when He first told the story.

When interpreting parables, it is important to discover the one central truth which the parable is designed to teach and base our interpretation on that fundamental principle. Usually, the context points to the interpretation. The Parable of the Good Samaritan was told in response to a question "Who is my neighbor?" (Luke 10:29). Jesus told this parable to answer that question. Therefore, our interpretation of this parable should focus on His answer. Care needs to be taken to interpret each part of the parable that needs to be explained in harmony with that answer.

Often an important step in discovering the primary focus of the parable is to consider how much of the parable is

NOT *Who is my neighbor?*
BUT *Am I neighborly?*

interpreted by Jesus Himself. On various occasions, Jesus explained His own stories in greater detail, often in response to questions from His disciples concerning the meaning of the parable. In the case of the Parable of the Good Samaritan, both the introduction and conclusion of the story suggest the primary interpretation which should be sought. Jesus concluded the story by asking the question, "So which of these three do you think was neighbor to him who fell among the thieves?" (Luke 10:36). That conclusion addresses the same subject raised by the lawyer which prompted the story.

If there is no clear interpretation given in Scripture, an attempt should be made to determine if there are other clues in the biblical context which might suggest the emphasis of the parable. To do this, you may need to research details about the customs and practices of that time and other matters raised in the story. When Jesus chose not to interpret His parables further, it was probably because they clearly understood what He said. When He told the Parable of the Sower and the Seed, everyone who heard it could picture the farmer scattering seed across his fields. Today, a prairie farmer may have difficulty understanding why that farmer got such a low percentage of return on his seed because he thinks of sowing seed using modern technology, which is more efficient than the Palestinian method of the first century. It is important to interpret parables in the historic context in which they were told, rather than impose our contemporary cultural models.

Balance is an important concept when it comes to interpreting parables. Many teachers err by interpreting too much of the parable, or by not interpreting enough of the story. As you study parables, work hard to avoid both of these extremes. First, don't make the parable walk on all fours. It is not necessary to force an interpretation of the parable on every point of the story. When Jesus said, "Consider the lilies of the field" (Matt. 6:28), He was not suggesting there were deeper truths hidden in each petal of each flower. Neither was there any apparent attempt to teach a spiritual lesson from the soil types in which lilies are most likely to grow. These details are like the drapery in a room, which gives background. Drapery is seldom the focus of a room. When we look at the way Jesus Himself interpreted the parables, it is clear that we should avoid this extreme of insisting on every aspect of the parable being interpreted for its "deeper meaning." Interpreting every point of a parable is like trying to make every part of a ball touch every part of a flat plane. When you do that, a ball is no longer a ball. Likewise, when we force every point of a parable, we no longer have a parable.

The second extreme to avoid in this matter is that of supposing that only the broadest issues of the parable should be interpreted. Sometimes, the context of a parable makes it clear that certain details are significant in the intended message. The Parable of the Sower and the Seed was apparently intended to tell us more than the basic message that the gospel seed should be sown widely in the world. Jesus Himself explained to His disciples the significance of four different types of soil in which the seed was sown. Jesus was suggesting there was truth to be learned in those details. In our zeal to avoid the extreme of finding hidden truth where truth was never hidden, let's be careful not to overreact and neglect the truth that has been included. In most cases, how much of the parable should be interpreted becomes clear as we consider the context carefully.

Ultimately, each parable has its own lesson which is based on the original intent of the Lord in telling the story. This meaning will be reinforced by the similarity between the story and the

> *"All the Bible is for all of us, but it is not all about us."*
>
> —*Graham Scroggie*

interpretation. But this similarity must be real, not imaginary. Interpretation is limited to the author's intent at the time of writing, but application shows us a current plan to obey and respond today.

There is only one interpretation to each parable. However, that interpretation may have many applications in different settings. The mature student knows the difference between application and interpretation.

> *Applications are many, principles are few; Applications may change, but principles never do.*

Perhaps one additional caution should be noted before concluding our discussion of this approach to Bible study. Be careful of the doctrinal use of parables. In the past, some biblical interpreters have made the mistake of using parables to teach new doctrine. It is unwise to form doctrinal conclusions on the basis of apparent implications suggested in a parable. It is important that doctrines look to the clear teaching of Scriptures such as the epistles or recorded sermons of Jesus. While a parable may be consistent with doctrine, don't make it the basis for doctrine. It is always best to draw doctrinal principles from the direct teaching of Scriptures. If a parable is referred to in a doctrinal study, it should not be considered as more than an illustration of the clear teaching of Scripture else-where.

PRINCIPLES FOR INTERPRETING A PARABLE

1. Determine the people included in the parable. What was characteristic of the individual, including how they lived out their purpose?
2. Determine how people used the things, customs, and practices that are described in the parable.
3. Determine the central truth of the parable and resist applying to your life many of the secondary aspects.
4. Begin with the Lord's interpretation of the parable and extend your study from there.
5. Look for clues about the interpretation in the events that led up to the parable.
6. Don't make a parable walk on all fours; don't press every detail for an interpretation or application.
7. Be careful of trying to prove doctrine from parables. They were given to illustrate.
8. Be careful of developing prophecy from parables because they usually illustrate predictions that are made elsewhere in Scripture.

How to Teach a Parable

While there are many different ways to teach biblical truth, there is one teaching method which lends itself particularly well to the teaching of parables. Teachers who teach parables often will want to master the art of storytelling. From generation to generation, culture to culture, deep abiding truths have been taught through stories that capture the imagination of the listener. Parables themselves are good examples of the powerful effect a good story can have on others.

When telling the stories of Jesus, care should be taken to capture the interest of your students quickly and maintain it throughout the story. While the stories of Jesus are interesting enough in themselves, many are so well known that people assume they already know all there is to know about the story. As soon as they begin to hear you talk about a man beaten on the road to Jerusalem, they know where you are going and may begin to tune you out. That's why it is important to remember the Disney principle of storytelling.

Walt Disney built an entertainment empire around the telling of stories. Many of the Disney company's most significant hits were stories which had been told for years before Disney began telling them. So how did Disney build the world's largest entertainment company with a bunch of old and familiar stories? The secret was creativity.

One of Disney's first great films was the story of Snow White. While many had told the story before, no one had ever done it before with animation. Telling "the same old story" in a new and different way has captured the imaginations of younger generations. Leading musicians, actors, and actresses count it a privilege to be the voice behind a cartoon caricature in a Disney feature film, and families line up to see the movie on the big screen or purchase the video as soon as it is released.

When teaching a parable, take time to retell the story in a creative setting or from a creative perspective. What would a Good Samaritan look like in your community? How would the lost sheep helplessly separated from the rest of the flock describe his rescue by a Good Shepherd? If coins could talk, how would the lost coin describe the housecleaning by a frantic woman from his perspective under a couch?

Sometimes, creativity can be achieved through costumes and/or drama in recounting the facts of a story. As part of a lesson on the Parable of the Prodigal Son, a teacher might arrange for others to re-enact the story to help people better visualize what is taking place. Sometimes the study group itself might prepare a drama based on a parable to be part of a special program at a local nursing home. Another teacher might want to interview the primary character described in a parable.

One problem with creativity is that it is only creative when it is fresh. No matter how well your approach to a story works this week, it will lose its effectiveness quickly if it is the only approach you use. Variety is the key to maintaining your creativity in teaching. By using different approaches to tell different stories each week, you can continue to capture the interest of your students week after week.

While creativity will help you communicate the facts of the story in an entertaining way, as a teacher you are interested in doing more than simply sharing content. Your ultimate aim is to change lives. This can only be done as you take time to apply the story to the life experience of those you teach. As you tell the story, be sure to tell what it means. Different teachers do this in different ways. Some pause momentarily at various points in the story to emphasize a specific principle that needs to be learned by the students. Others wait until the end of the story to emphasize several important principles which can be drawn out of the story. The means by which you help those you are teaching identify the specific truths hidden in the parable will depend upon the approach you feel most comfortable with and that which your students respond to best.

Once the principles have been communicated, help your students make specific application in their lives by adopting an appropriate project. For some Bible study groups, it would be appropriate for a study of the Parable of the Good Samaritan to conclude with a challenge to prepare Christmas gift baskets for families of prisoners. Another group might find value calling those who have been absent from church in recent weeks in response to their study of the Parable of the Lost Sheep. In teaching the parables, as in all Bible study, it is important that we help our students become more than hearers only, but also doers of the Word of God.

Tools for Studies in the Parables

If you study and teach parables on a regular basis, you may want to invest in a few good books on the parables. These books will serve as reference tools in the process of your own studies of the stories of Jesus. While not exhaustive, the following list identifies several leading books in this field.

Barclay, William. *And Jesus Said: A Handbook on the Parables of Christ*. Philadelphia: Westminster/John Knox, 1971.

Dods, Marcus. *The Parables of Our Lord*. London: Hodder & Stoughton, 1894.

Lockyer, Herbert. *All the Parables of the Bible*. Grand Rapids: Zondervan Publishing House, 1963.

Morgan, G. Campbell. *The Parables and Metaphors of Our Lord*. New York: Fleming H. Revell, 1943.

A Study of the Parable of the Good Samaritan
Luke 10:25–37

1. Who was talking with Jesus when the parable was given, and what was the motivation for the parable?

> *"A certain lawyer stood up and tested him (Jesus)" (Luke 10:25). "Woe to you lawyers! For you have taken away the key of knowledge. You did not enter in yourselves, and those who were entering in you hindered" (Luke 11:52).*

2. Was the lawyer's question sincere?

> *"Teacher, what shall I do to inherit eternal life?" (Luke 10:26).*

3. Jesus told him to look in the law. What are the two answers found there?

> *"You shall love the Lord your God with all your heart, with all your soul, with all your mind, and your neighbor as yourself" (Luke 10:27, 28).*

4. Why did the lawyer ask a second question?

> *"But he (the lawyer), wanting to justify himself, said to Jesus, 'And who is my neighbor?'" (Luke 10:28).*

5. List the six people in the parable? (Luke 10:30–35).

6. What are the three main problems in the parable?

"A certain man . . . fell among thieves, who stripped him of his clothing, wounding him" (v. 30). "A certain priest . . . passed by on the other side" (v. 31). "A Levite . . . passed by on the other side" (v. 32). "Take care of him, and whatsoever more you send . . . I will repay" (v. 35).

7. What actions did the Samaritan take?

"He [the Samaritan] saw him, he had compassion . . . went to him . . . bandaged his wounds, pouring on oil . . . sat him on his own animal, brought him to an inn" (v. 33, 34).

8. How did the Samaritans and Jews get along?

"How is it that you [Jesus] being a Jew, ask a drink from me, a Samaritan woman? For the Jews have no dealings with Samaritans" (John 4:9).

9. Why did Jesus ask the lawyer to interpret the parable?

"So which of these three do you think was neighbor to him who fell among the thieves?" (v. 36).

10. What was Jesus asking the lawyer to do?

Jesus said to him, "Go and do likewise" (v. 37).

Bible Study Application

A Checklist for Studying Parables

1. Name of the parable

   Bible reference

2. List the persons involved

3. List the places involved

4. Give other details—time, objects, conditions

5. What was the background that motivated the parable?

6. Summarize the story.

7. What are the parallel items between the story and the application?

8. What interpretation is given by the teller of the parable?

9. What is the main point?

10. What practical application can you apply to your life?

CHAPTER SIX

STUDYING A CHAPTER OR BOOK FROM THE BIBLE

"Where are my keys?" the man called out as he frantically looked in several of the usual places he might have left them. "I can't find them, and I'm going to be late for work!" he exclaimed in frustration.

"Have you checked your coat pocket?" his wife asked, trying to be helpful.

"Oh!" was the simple response after he thrust his hand into his pocket and felt the collection of keys.

The Best Way to Study the Bible

Sometimes, in our zeal to find things, we end up looking everywhere but the obvious places. That happens with keys, shoes, books, even Bible study. While there are many ways to study the Bible, we need to be careful not to avoid studying our Bible in the most obvious way. According to William Evans,

> The best method of the study of any organism is that which gives due prominence to the structure of that organism. The Bible is a living organism of truth; it has in it the life of the living God and is able (as no other book is) to impart spiritual life to the soul of man. The Bible was made bookwise —one book at a time, according as the need for the truth, historical, prophetical or ethical, as set forth therein, arose. It would seem reasonable, therefore, to assume that the book-method of Bible study should yield the best results from time and labor spent in an endeavor to "search the Scriptures."[1]

As a young man beginning his pastoral ministry, Dr. W. A. Criswell was invited to pastor an older church and follow one of the most famous pastors of his day. Sensing something of the significance of the challenge he was facing, Criswell talked with other pastors and asked them for their advice as he began this new phase of his ministry. Someone advised him his best course would be to begin in Genesis and preach through the Bible over a period of many years. As Criswell followed this advice, he found people were hungry to study the Scriptures. By the time he retired from the pulpit of First Baptist Church in Dallas, Texas, that church had become the largest of all Southern Baptist churches. His success in teaching the Bible book-by-book and chapter-by-chapter has motivated many other pastors to adopt his example as their primary preaching style. Many of these men are also experiencing steady long-term growth in their ministries. People are still hungry to study the Scriptures.

Why Study the Bible by Chapter and Book?

There are several good reasons to study and teach the Bible, book-by-book and chapter-by-chapter. For many Christians, this is the most obvious way to read and study the Scriptures. They plan their daily devotions around the unspoken principle, "A chapter a day keeps the devil away." While it is good to get into the habit of Bible study, you need other reasons to keep you motivated.

As noted above, one good reason for studying the Bible by books is that the Bible was written in books. Each of the sixty-six books of the Bible has a particular emphasis and/or theme. When the prophet first preached his sermons or an apostle first wrote a letter, they were trying to communicate a specific thought or theme. These themes are best understood in the context of the whole content of the book. When we study the Bible by book, we learn the major lessons of the Scripture in the manner which the human authors of Scripture intended to teach them.

Though added some time after the Scriptures were complete, chapters tend to break larger books down into more manageable sections for Bible study. The student of Isaiah might be overwhelmed trying to study through the entire book, but can be challenged to study chapter six in greater detail—where Isaiah saw the Lord and received a commission to preach and write. In the Old Testament, the average chapter is just under twenty-five verses long. That compares to just over thirty verses in length in the New Testament. While the student of the Scriptures might want to break some longer chapters into smaller units (Psalm 119, for example), most find the average chapter about the right length for a challenging Bible study.

Taking a chapter approach to Bible study is not just practical, it is also a logical way to learn the principal teachings of the Scriptures.

Several key chapters of the Bible actually summarize key thoughts or doctrines of the Bible. One effective approach to the doctrinal study of the Scriptures involves a thorough study of these key passages. The following chart identifies a few of those chapters and the doctrines and/or themes they address.

STUDYING KEY THEMES IN KEY CHAPTERS

The Creation of the World in Genesis 1
The Fall of Humanity in Genesis 3
The Ethical Code of the Law in Exodus 20
The Lord as Our Shepherd in Psalm 23
The Suffering Saviour in Isaiah 53
The New Birth in John 3
The Founding of the Church in Acts 2
The Nature of Love in 1 Corinthians 13
The Doctrine of the Resurrection in 1 Corinthians 15
The Nature of Faith in Hebrews 11
The Kingdom of Christ in Revelation 20

The study of the Bible by book and chapter provides a context in which the various details or verses of Scripture can be better understood. Many Christians have an understanding of various isolated passages in the Scripture, but have never learned how they fit together. When we study the Bible book-by-book, we begin to understand the broader context of each book. Almost everyone knows John 3:16, but do they know John's purpose was to demonstrate the deifying Christ so people could believe and live (John 20:31)? When a book approach is coupled with the study of the Scriptures chapter-by-chapter, the finer details of Scripture are understood in their biblical context.

OWNING A BOOK

1. *Study the facts of the book.*
2. *Analyze the individual facts to understand the book's general focus and structure.*
3. *Compare the structure of the book to each section to determine the author's purpose of writing.*
4. *Write an outline of the book in your own words.*
5. *Determine and mark the key verse, the verse that best reflects the author's purpose.*
6. *Determine the key word, and mark each occurrence in the book.*
7. *Think through the general truth to applying them to your life.*

How to Study a Book and Chapter of the Bible

As we consider studying the Scriptures by book and chapter, the logical place to begin is by choosing and surveying a specific biblical book. This is sometimes called the synthetic approach to Bible study. Merrill C. Tenney described it in these words:

> The interpretation of a book in its totality by such a process of repeated reading and final integration of results is called the synthetic method. The word *synthetic* is derived from the Greek preposition *syn,* which means together, and the verbal root *the,* which means to put, so that the resultant meaning is "a putting together." Synthetic is the opposite of analytic, which means "a taking apart." The synthetic method ignores detail, and treats only of the interpretation of a document as a whole.[2]

While any of the sixty-six books of the Bible can be studied synthetically, the size of a biblical book is a practical consideration, especially for those who are studying the Bible for the first time. The student who attempts to learn this method of Bible study by using a book of the Pentateuch, one of the major prophets, a gospel or one of the longer New Testament epistles in his or her first attempt at Bible study is likely to encounter unnecessary difficulty. A better approach is to choose one of the smaller books in Scripture for the first few attempts while learning this method, then later apply the method to larger books when you are more familiar with this approach. The following chart identifies some of the shorter books in the Bible which should be considered as you begin studying the Bible book-by-book.

THE SHORTER BOOKS OF THE BIBLE

Ruth	Joel	Jonah
Haggai	Habakkuk	Zephaniah
Malachi	Philippians	Colossians
2 Thessalonians	2 Timothy	Titus
2 Peter		

The shortest books of the Bible are also called the one-chapter books. The New Testament one-chapter books were actually letters that correspond in length to those we might write.

ONE-CHAPTER BOOKS OF THE BIBLE

Obadiah	Philemon	2 John
3 John	Jude	

As you begin studying one of these books, attempt to determine the probable historical context. Before you can understand and apply the Bible to your life, it is important to know how those who first heard it would have understood its message. To learn more about the historical context of the book, there are several questions you can ask. Begin with questions about the author of the book. Who wrote this book? What is known about this author? Then ask about the book itself. Why was this book written? How does the original purpose of this book relate to my life today? Next ask about those who first read this book. To whom was this book originally written? What similarities do I share with the original recipients of the book? How are we different? You may want to consider the uniqueness of your book with others written by the same author or about the same time. How does this book relate to other books by this author? How does it relate to other books written about this time? Finally, consider the context of the times in which this book was produced. When was this book written? What significant things were happening in the world at the time when this book was originally written?

FROM ONE WORD TO KNOW ALL THE WORD

Understand each word in a verse.
Relate the verse in its paragraph.
See how the paragraph fits into the chapter.
Connect chapter to understand a book.
Compare books to group the whole Bible.

Set aside time to read the book through without interruption. You may have to put your telephone on the answering machine to minimize the chance of interruption. Some people choose to leave their house and read their Bible in a quiet neighborhood park. Reading through the book this way will help you get a feel for the basic structure of the book.

Actually, you will want to do this several times. In your first reading, look for the central theme of the book and how the author develops it. Next, look for key words and circle them in your Bible. Look for a key verse or pivotal passage in the book. You might want to circle them. In your next reading, look for ways the central theme is emphasized in the book. In another reading, begin developing a summary outline of the book. Give each chapter a brief title that summarizes its main message. In subsequent readings, expand your book outline. You may want to write a three-to-five-word summary of each paragraph; some even write these in their Bible at the heading of a chapter.

Reading through a book of the Bible four or five times as part of your Bible study may seem like an ambitious undertaking, but the benefits are far greater than the work involved. Before preaching from any chapter in the New Testament, G. Campbell Morgan read the entire book from which that chapter was taken forty times, in Greek. As a result, he earned the reputation of being one of the outstanding Bible teachers of his day. As you read your book several times, you may want to read from various translations. This will help you approach each reading fresh as each translation expresses the message in a slightly different manner. Also, reading your book through once each day for seven days will produce better results than reading it though seven consecutive times on one day.

By the time you have read through the book several times, you should have a fairly clear understanding of the book. Because you want to be both a hearer and doer of the Word, the next step involves comparing the theme of the book to your life. Does the book suggest specific actions to take? Does the book suggest a specific value or attitude to adopt? How does this book expand my understanding of God and the Christian life?

Once you have completed your study of a book, you may want to follow it up with a series of chapter studies to gain a better understanding of each chapter in the context of the broader message of the book. There are three additional steps involved in completing a chapter study.

The first step involves observing the details of the chapter being studied. Once again, asking the right questions is the key to gaining the right answers in your pursuit of a better understanding of the Scriptures. Use the following dozen questions to guide you to a better understanding of each chapter. (1) Who are the prominent characters in this chapter? (2) How are these characters related to each other? (3) What is the major event in this chapter? (4) How is this event related to other minor events mentioned? (5) When do the events of this chapter take place? (6) What was happening in the world when these things happened? (7) What events were taking place just before and/or after the events described in this chapter? (8) Where do these events take place? List each place mentioned and find them in a good Bible atlas. (9) Why does the writer express himself as he does in this chapter? (10) What motives lie behind the actions taken in this chapter? (11) How does the author describe the people, places, and events in this chapter? (12) What significance is there in the way these things are described?

The next step involves determining the meaning of the chapter. To do this, you will analyze each paragraph in the chapter. To gain a good understanding of the chapter, write a three-to-five-word summary of each paragraph unit within the chapter. Then make a list of words you do not understand. Look up each of these words in a Bible dictionary. To ensure you have a good understanding of the chapter's contents, write a paraphrase of the chapter in your own words that clearly communicates the meaning of the chapter.

The ultimate goal of Bible study is a changed life. So, determine how the principles of this chapter can be best applied to your life. The following five questions may help guide you as you look for an appropriate application of this chapter to your life. (1) Is there an example to follow? (2) Is there a command to obey? (3) Is there a promise to claim? (4) Is there a prayer to pray? (5) Is there an error to avoid?

PRINCIPLES FOR STUDYING A CHAPTER

1. The Bible must be interpreted with a view that God is speaking to us through every chapter. Determine if a chapter is historical, poetic, didactic, a sermon, biography, etc.
2. Study the chapter to determine the historical background to which it is addressed.
3. Determine the meaning of proper names, events, things, geographical places, and customs.
4. What unusual words are used in the chapter, and how does their meaning help to interpret the chapter?
5. Determine why the author has included this chapter in Scripture by asking what is its focus or point.
6. After a chapter has been studied, determine what principles are evident in the passage and how can they be applied to your life.
7. Your interpretation will basically support the solid accepted views of Bible students in the body of Christ, because no Scripture is of "private interpretation."

How to Teach the Bible By Chapter and Book

When the focus of a Bible study session is a chapter or book of the Bible, remember that your students must group the message of the book or chapter before they can apply it to their lives. When surveyed, about half of those involved in Bible study groups said they preferred doing a book study in their Bible study group. Most were not simply interested in expanding their biblical knowledge; rather, they wanted to study the Bible itself to apply it to their lives. Therefore, when we teach a chapter or book of the Bible, it is important to demonstrate how these ancient writings guide us today.

Begin your Bible study session by introducing your chapter or book study by drawing attention to the theme of the chapter or book. You may want to ask an opinion question which leads group members to express their own views about the theme. On another occasion, introduce a quote by a prominent person or from a popular song that deals with the theme. Then ask group members to respond to that quote. Some Bible teachers prefer to write the word that describes the theme on the chalkboard and ask group members what they think about when they see or hear that word used.

TEACHING THE BIBLE BY BOOKS

The Romance of Redemption . . . Ruth
The Providence of God in the Affairs of people . . . Esther
The Struggles of a Racist Prophet . . . Jonah
The Acts of the Holy Spirit . . . Acts
Christ is Better . . . Hebrews

Next, introduce the book being studied in the context of the theme, as illustrated in the chart above. Then lead your students through your book outline, focusing on how the author develops that theme. Your goal in approaching the book this way is to help your students begin to recognize the message of the book for itself. When you are teaching a chapter, you will want to follow a similar procedure. As you lead the class discussion, encourage group members to suggest ways the author develops that theme in the chapter (see *Studying Key Themes in Key Chapters* chart earlier in this chapter).

As you teach this lesson, list the basic principles emphasized in the book or chapter being studied. Is there an example to follow? Is there a command to obey? Is there a promise to claim? Is there a prayer to pray? Is there an error to avoid?

Your goal in teaching the Bible is to lead your students to apply the Bible. Ask group members to identify specific steps they can take this week to apply one principle to their life. Everyone who has made a New Year's resolution or decided to lose weight knows intentions are not good enough on their own. People don't do what is expected; they do what is *inspected.* Therefore, have your Bible study group members share these steps with other group members who will hold them accountable for their actions this week.

Often, a book study is followed by a series of chapter studies from the same book in Bible-based curricula. Also, many teachers who teach a chapter study do so as part of an extended series taking students through a biblical book. If your study is part of a similar series, be sure to assign a chapter or book to be read by group members in preparation for the next group Bible study session. This will make it that much easier for you as you continue teaching the Bible book-by-book and chapter-by-chapter.

Tools for Book and Chapter Studies

If you study and teach the Bible by book and chapter on a regular basis, you may want to invest in a few good books on biblical introduction and some commentaries. These books will serve as reference tools in the process of developing your own book and chapter studies. While not exhaustive, the following list identifies several leading nontechnical books in this field.

Ironside, H. A. Various Commentaries. Neptune, N.J.: Loizeaux Brothers.

LaSor, William Sanford, David Allan Hubbard, and Frederic William Bush. *Old Testament Survey: The Message, Form, and Background of the Old Testament.* Grand Rapids: William B. Eerdmans Publishing Company, 1994.

Morris, Leon, ed. *The Tyndale Commentaries.* Grand Rapids: William B. Eerdmans Publishing Company.

Motyer, J. A. Motyer, John R. W. Stott, eds. *The Bible Speaks Today* series. Downers Grove, Ill.: Intervarsity Press.

Tenney, Merrill C. *New Testament Survey.* Grand Rapids: Wm. B. Erdmans Publishing Co., 1972.

Wiersbe, Warren W. *Be Series Commentaries.* Wheaton, Ill.: Victor Books.

A Book and Chaper Bible Study Philemon 1–25

1. How are the people in this book related to each other?

   > Onesimus (name means profitable) was a slave, who robbed his master Philemon and fled to Rome. There he was converted under the ministry of Paul, who now sends Onesimus back to Philemon with this letter.

   Onesimus to Philemon. "Who [Onesimus] once was unprofitable to you, but now is profitable to you and to me" (v. 11).

   Philemon to Paul. "I appeal to you for my son, Onesimus whom I have begotten while in my chains" (v. 10).

   Paul to Philemon. "I [Paul] am sending him back. You therefore receive him" (v. 12).

2. What past connection had Paul to Philemon?

   > "I, Paul, am writing this with my own hand . . . not to mention to you that you owe me even your own self beside" (v. 19).

Bible Study Application

3. What was Philemon's position in the church?

> "Paul, . . . to Philemon our beloved friend and fellow laborer . . . and to the church in your house" (v. 1, 2).

4. What was Paul's condition when writing?

> "Paul, a prisoner of Christ Jesus" (v. 1). "I have begotten [Onesimus] while in my chains" (v. 10). "I wish to keep (Onesimus) with me . . . he might minister to me in my chains" (v. 13).

5. What was Paul's motive in asking forgiveness for Onesimus?

> "I might be very bold in Christ to command you what is fitting, yet for love's sake, I rather appeal to you" (v. 8, 9). "That your good deed might not be by compulsion . . . but voluntary" (v. 14).

6. What did Paul think Onesimus would do for Philemon?

> "He departed for a while [escaped] . . . that you might receive him forever, no longer as a slave, but more than as a slave, as a beloved brother" (v. 15, 16).

7. On what basis did Paul want Onesimus received back?

> "If you count me as a partner, receive him as you would me, but if he has wronged you or owes you anything, put that on my account" (v. 17, 18).

8. What has Christ
   done for you?

   What could the
   Father do?

   What is your
   response?

> We are like Onesimus who has sinned against God. Philemon is a picture of God who has the authority to punish us. Paul is a picture of Christ and says, "Put his sin on my account."

9. What results does
   Paul expect from
   this letter?

> "Having confidence in your obedience, I [Paul] write to you, knowing that you will do even more than I say" (v. 21).

Bible Study Application

A Checklist for Studying a Bible Chapter and Book

Name of book

Key word

Key verse

Why is this word/verse key to the passage?

Who wrote it?

Why did he write it?

To whom was it written?

Where was it written?

When was it written?

What was the problem?

What answers were suggested?

What principles were included?

What practical suggestions were given?

List the characters and one statement about each.

CHAPTER SEVEN

STUDYING A STORY/NARRATIVE

Everyone loves a good story, and no one can tell a good story like a good storyteller. One of the greatest storytellers of all time was Charles Dickens. His writings are recognized classics, and most English-speaking people have read one of his books, or at least watched a movie based on one of his stories. His book, *A Christmas Carol*, has made Ebenezer Scrooge a part of the Christmas culture of the western world.

Although millions consider his novels among the best books ever written, Charles Dickens had a different idea. Concerning the Bible, he said, "It is the best Book that ever was or ever will be in the world."

Dickens' opinion is shared by many other students of literature who may or may not share an evangelical view of the Scriptures as the Word of God. Students of the mystery novel in college are often introduced to the greatest mystery ever written, the Book of Job. The moving drama of Ruth or Esther captures the minds and hearts of readers.

The stories from Joshua, Judges, and the histories of the kings of Israel and Judah rival the plots of the best adventure movies ever produced. In the New Testament, the gospels and Acts are full of great stories describing the real-life adventures and experiences of Jesus, the apostles, and many others who influenced history.

In another chapter, we considered how to study and teach a parable. Parables are stories which were not recollections of actual events, but were stories based on the everyday events of Jesus' day. In this chapter, we will consider how to study and teach a biblical narrative. You will study real-life adventure stories and personal dramas of Scripture.

Why Study Bible Stories?

All Scripture is inspired and profitable—and that includes biblical narratives. Reminding his readers about the experiences of Israel in the wilderness, Paul wrote, "Now these things became our examples, to the intent that we should not lust after evil things as they also lusted" (1 Cor. 10:6). His conclusion was not intended to be applied only to those living in the first century. He later repeated this claim by noting, "Now all these things happened to them as examples, and they were written for our admonition, upon whom the ends of the ages have come" (1 Cor. 10:11). We are the ones upon "whom the ages have come."

From time to time, all of us get discouraged. One way to address the problem of discouragement is to review what God has done in the past. Considering the victories God worked at other times can encourage us in the midst of difficult times. The psalmist Asaph used this strategy to prevent "the blues" from becoming "the blahs." In the midst of an anguishing experience, he wrote, "I will remember the works of the LORD; surely I will remember Your wonders of old. I will also meditate on all Your work, and talk of Your deeds" (Ps. 77:11, 12).

The study of biblical narratives can also help Christians grow in their faith. The Jewish people were held responsible by God to tell their children the stories of how God worked throughout their history "that they may set their hope in God and not forget the works of God, but keep His commandments" (Ps. 78:7). Reviewing what God has done for others serves to strengthen our faith and hope in God.

The study of biblical narratives also helps us develop a spirit of thanksgiving toward God. God wants His people to be grateful (Psalm 100:4). Reviewing what God did for others helps us recognize His intervention in our lives and serves as a basis for thanksgiving. In one of the Sabbath psalms of the Old Testament, the worshiper declared, "For You, LORD, have made me glad through Your work; I will triumph in the works of Your hands" (Ps. 92:4).

One of the things God looks for in His people is worship. "The Father seeketh such to worship Him" (John 4:23). Reviewing what God has done in the past causes us to celebrate Him and His mighty works. David wrote, "I will praise You, for I am fearfully and wonderfully made; marvellous are Your works, and that my soul knows very well" (Ps. 139:14). Celebrating God for His person and His works is the very essence of Christian worship.

How to Study a Biblical Narrative

Most people will find biblical narratives among the more interesting portions of Scripture. Everyone likes a story. Stories are easier to remember than theory or principles. However, people's interest in stories may or may not be translated into the effort needed to study a passage in greater detail. This will be especially true if the narrative covers several chapters. As you begin studying narratives in Bible study, limit the size of the story you are studying. You will find initial attempts using this method more beneficial if you limit yourself to the account of some specific battle or event than a larger study such as the plagues of Egypt or story of Esther. Once you become more familiar with using this method, you will also find it helpful in larger studies.

Having selected the account you are studying, begin by surveying the narrative to gain a "feel" for the event being described. Ask yourself several questions to help you better understand what is taking place.

- Who are the major characters ?
- What plot unfolds?
- How much time passes?

As you consider these details, you will find yourself coming away with new insights on a familiar story.

Next, consider the narrative passage in its broader context.

- How does this passage fit into the book in which it is found?
- Why did the author include it in his account?
- How does this passage fit into the history of the people, nations, and/or cause ?
- What has previously happened to make this event possible?
- How do previous events set up the events to unfold in the story?

These questions will help you see beyond the story itself and place the narrative in a meaningful context.

A third step in understanding the story itself involves setting this event in its historical and geographic context.

- Who were the rulers of this age?
- How do these leaders influence what is happening in the story?
- What special feasts or festivals were being celebrated in the seasons mentioned?

Just as Christmas influences our society during the Christmas season, so the feasts of Israel had a similar, perhaps even stronger, influence on that society. As you are looking at the story from a historical and geographic perspective, find the places mentioned in the account in a good Bible atlas.

Give careful attention to the details of the account as you read it. Remember Rudyard Kippling's advice and probe for details using his "six serving men."

1. Who?

2. What?

3. Where?

4. When?

5. Why?

6. How?

You may want to rewrite the account as a contemporary news story reporting all the facts. Then check your story to ensure you have included all the data in the biblical account. On other occasions, you may want to lay out an analytical chart of the passage being studied that demonstrates relationships within the text. Both of these methods will help you better understand the details of the account.

Next, look for the significant lessons implied in this narrative. Once again, asking questions will help you gain a better understanding of the passage:

- Do the people involved demonstrate unique character qualities that should be copied or avoided?
- Does the action illustrate a proverb or other biblical principle?
- Does the narrative account suggest a historical context in which some other part of Scripture could be better understood?

Some of the psalms, sermons of Jesus, and epistles of Paul are best understood in the historical context of events that were happening at the time these things were said and/or written.

Studying some biblical narratives requires us to consult parallel accounts in other parts of the Bible to get a different perspective on the story. The Chronicles retell from the perspective of priests many events described in the books of Samuel and Kings that are given from the perspective of kings and prophets. Sometimes, new insights can be found concerning the reigns of various kings. Many events in the life of Christ are recorded in more than one gospel. Once again, one gospel writer may include details overlooked by the others. Many significant biblical events are retold by later writers, usually as part of a sermon attempting to define some specific principle. The crossing of the Red Sea may be the most familiar biblical event retold throughout the Scriptures.

As you conclude your study, look for ways the lessons can be applied to your life.

- Is there an attitude to be developed or dealt with in light of this account?

- Is there an action to be practiced or halted in light of this account?

The teacher must first learn the lesson before he or she can effectively teach it to others.

PRINCIPLES OF INTERPRETING A BIBLE STORY

1. Determine the climate, history, geography, businesses, and living conditions where the story took place.
2. Determine the main characteristics of people in the story.
3. Determine the people who acted and those who reacted.
4. Look behind the words of the conversation to the meaning of their messages.
5. Determine the positive principles in the story that can be applied and the negative principles to be avoided.
6. What contextual conditions/promises applied only to the characters of the story, and what universal principle can be applied to you today?

How to Teach a Bible Story

When teaching a biblical narrative, one of your goals is to help students become involved in the drama of the event itself. You want them to become as involved in the account you are studying as they might be watching a good movie or favorite television program. The more they understand the meaning of what is happening and can feel the same emotions of the primary characters in the account feel, the greater the likelihood they will learn the lesson God intended in recording this event.

Vary Your Approach

Helping your students become involved in the drama begins as you tell the story. Consider creative ways to capture the interest of your students in the biblical passage. You can do this in several ways. Some teachers ask a question that is embedded in the plot of the story to come. Others may use drama or period costumes to create an interest on the part of the students. Still other teachers highlight parts of the story to come to create interest on the part of the students. Some teachers might give the conclusion of the story, then ask what conditions led up to that conclusion.

As you plan your lesson, give thought to the best way to communicate the contents of your narrative. Sometimes it is best to retell the events in chronological order, dividing the narrative into a series of dramatic scenes. On other occasions, it may be better to begin with a dramatic climax and then resort to a flashback to explain how common events moved to such a place. Occasionally you may choose to focus on the major character in the account and teach the narrative as a partial character study. This third approach is described further in chapter two as a means of teaching a biblical biography (see pages 33-51).

Spice It Up

One way to maintain interest in your study sessions involves using a variety of teaching methods to communicate your lesson on a biblical narrative. Variety has been called "the spice of life." Just as a good cook adds a little spice to flavor the food, so a good teacher uses variety to improve the interest quotient in the lesson. But new teachers need to learn from good cooks before they begin tampering with their lesson plans. It is not the addition of spice to the food that makes it taste better, but rather the addition of the *right* spice and the right *amount* of spice that gives the meal a richer taste. Different foods require different spices.

How can a teacher know which new teaching methods to use in a specific teaching session? You should consider several factors in making this decision:

1. Consider the uniqueness of your students. Differences in age, sex, ethnic background, and other similar factors tend to suggest teaching methods which may be more appropriate.

2. Consider your own abilities as a teacher. Each teacher tends to feel more comfortable using some methods over others. While this is a very important consideration, don't use it as an excuse for expanding your horizons and moving out of your personal comfort zone.

3. Consider the resources available to you. Some teaching methods such as using films, videos, and audio tapes require equipment you may or may not have available.

4. Consider what you have been doing recently. Even the best teaching methods become less effective when used all the time.

Identify and Apply Principles

As you work through the lesson, highlight the significant principles to be drawn from the event described in this narrative.
- Is there a bad example to avoid?
- Is there a positive example to imitate?
- Is there a guiding principle or proverb that seems to govern the course of events in this account?

Remember, these things were written for us as our examples. If we fail to learn from the examples of others, we may find ourselves studying in the School of Hard Knocks.

As you guide those in your Bible study group toward making personal application, suggest ways this principle can be applied in their lives. As noted above, this begins with the teacher applying the lesson to his or her own life. Ask yourself some of the hard questions to identify how the principle relates to you:

- How does this principle affect my relationships?
- How does this principle change my attitudes about . . .?
- How should this principle change my character?
- How will this principle help me accomplish some worthy goal?

As the lesson becomes real in your life, these same questions can be used to help it become real in the lives of those you teach.

Bring It Down to Earth

Once you have identified how this principle can be applied in the lives of your Bible study group members, the next step in applying the lesson is to encourage group members to suggest practical ways this principle can be applied in a specific and relevant contemporary setting.

- What aspects of our contemporary lifestyle and experiences tend to parallel the kind of things described in this narrative?
- How would this eternal principle of God be expressed in the kind of cultural setting where we live today?
- What situations are members of your Bible study group likely to face in the next two weeks where this principle could be applied?

- What actions need to be taken to ensure group members respond correctly in a similar situation in their life?

Someone once said, "The only thing people learn from history is that people don't learn from history." That is certainly not God's intent in recording the history of His working among His people. As we teach the narrative passages of Scripture, our goal is to help others learn from His-story.

Tools for Narrative Studies

If you study and teach narrative passages on a regular basis, you may want to invest in a few good books dealing with Bible backgrounds, culture, and archaeology. These books will serve as reference tools in the process of studying biblical narratives. While not exhaustive, the following list identifies several leading books in this field. You may also want to consider some of the commentaries listed in chapter 6.

Crockett, William Day. *A Harmony of the Books of Samuel, Kings, and Chronicles: The Books of the Kings of Judah and Israel.* Grand Rapids: Baker Book House, 1971.

Harrison, R. K. *Old Testament Times.* Grand Rapids: William B. Eerdmans Publishing Company, 1970.

Livingston, Herbert G. *The Pentateuch in Its Cultural Environment.* Grand Rapids: Baker Book House, 1974.

Orr, James, ed. *International Standard Bible Encyclopedia.* Grand Rapids: Wm. B. Eerdmans Publishing Co., 1974.

Reese, Edward, ed. *The Chronological Bible.* Nashville: E. E. Gaddy & Associates, 1977.

Robertson, A. T. *A Harmony of the Gospels for Students of the Life of Christ.* San Francisco: HarperCollins, 1922.

Tenney, Merrill C. *New Testament Times.* Grand Rapids: Wm. B. Eerdmans Publishing Co., 1972.

Unger, Merrill F. *Unger's Bible Handbook.* Chicago: Moody Press, 1957.

BIBLE STUDY ON THE MIRACULOUS CATCH OF 153 FISH
John 21:1–14

1. What were the conditions of the story?

> "Jesus showed Himself again to His disciples at the Sea of Galilee" (v. 1). Read about the Sea of Galilee in a Bible dictionary. "This is now the third time Jesus showed Himself to His disciples after He was raised from the dead" (v. 14).

2. List the people in the story.

> "Simon Peter, Thomas called Didymus, Nathanael of Cana in Galilee, the sons of Zebedee, and two other of His disciples" (v. 2). "Jesus stood on the shore" (v. 4).

3. What were the two crises in the story?

> "I am going fishing . . . "We are going with you . . . that night they caught nothing" (v. 3). "Cast the net on the right side of the boat and you will find some" (v. 6).

4. What natural conditions kept the disciples from recognizing Jesus?

> "When the morning had now come" (v. 4). "They were not far from land, about 100 yards" (v. 8). "That disciple . . . said to Peter, 'It is the Lord!' "(v. 7).

5. What spiritual conditions might have kept the disciples from recognizing Jesus?

> "But their eyes (2 disciples on road to Emmaus) were restrained, so that they did not know Him" (Luke 24:16). "Then their eyes were opened and they knew Him" (Luke 24:31).

6. What are some natural and spiritual conditions that keep you from seeing Christ in your life?

7. What were the 2 different responses to Christ?

> "That disciple whom Jesus loved (John) said to Peter, 'It is the Lord!' When Simon Peter heard it was the Lord, he put on his outer garment . . . and plunged into the sea" (v. 7).

8. How is your faith—insightful or impulsive?

9. How had Christ prepared for their needs?

> "As soon as they were come to land, they saw a fire of coals there, and fish laid on it, and bread" (v. 9). "Come and eat breakfast" (v. 12).

10. How has Christ prepared for your needs?

11. What happened when Christ appeared to them?

> "None of the disciples dare ask Him, 'Who are You?'—knowing that it was the Lord" (v. 12).

12. How does Christ make Himself real to you?

Bible Study Application

A Checklist for Studying a Bible Story

1.   References

2.   Speaker/Date

3.   Place where story was given

4.   People in the story

5.   Give other details—time, objects, conditions

6.   What was the background that motivated the story?

7.   Summarize the events and story line.

8.   Why was the story given?

9.   What is the main point of the story?

10.   What would we miss if the story were not in Scripture?

11.   What practical application can you apply to your life?

CHAPTER EIGHT

STUDYING PROPHECY

What did Japanese Emperor Hirohito, Italian Dictator Benito Mussolini, German Dictator Adolph Hitler, British King Henry VIII, American President John F. Kennedy, Cuban ruler Fidel Castro, and Russian leader Mikhail Gorbachev have in common with popular singers of their time Elvis Presley, John Lennon, Michael Jackson and every Roman Catholic pope since the Reformation? Someone, somewhere, has identified them conclusively as the Antichrist prophesied in Scripture. While none of it is true, people nevertheless continue to wrongly identify the Antichrist.

In 1988, a small book was published and widely distributed throughout North America that claimed to have solved, once and for all, one of the greatest prophetic mysteries of all time. The evangelist/author of the book listed "eighty-eight reasons why the rapture will be in 1988." The conclusions of his extensive research were that the rapture of the church would take place in September 1988 during the Jewish feast of Rosh Hoshana and that Christ would ultimately return to earth during the Yom Kippur celebrations of 1995. Although the book sold well, there was at least one major flaw . . . it didn't happen!

A few years ago, a popular evangelical leader in South Korea gathered a large following when he too announced the return of the Lord on a specific October date. Because the end was near, many of his followers sold their homes below market value to raise funds to further the work of that ministry so the message could get out before it was too late. Like his North American counterpart, this Asian preacher proved to be wrong in his calculations. But the day after the Lord did not return as anticipated, things got worse for the South Korean false prophet. The police arrested him. They wanted to know why he had been purchasing the property of his church members with ministry funds when he had expected the end of the world. Good question!

Why Study Bible Prophecy?

With the many abuses of prophecy all around us, it is easy to become cynical about the study of prophecy. But if you do so, you neglect a significant dimension of personal Bible study that could be a blessing to you. Also, you limit your teaching ministry unnecessarily. There are good reasons for studying Bible prophecy and valid principles to govern your study of these Scriptures. When applied consistently, you can be an effective teacher of Bible prophecy while avoiding some of the more common abuses we witness all around us.

1. *We must teach Bible prophecy to teach "the whole counsel of God."* Over one third of the Scriptures were prophetic when

written. When we fail to teach Bible prophecy, we are ignoring a major portion of the Word of God. We can't eliminate prophecy if we are committed to teaching the whole Bible. To neglect the teaching of Bible prophecy would be similar to refusing to teach from the New Testament. Anyone who takes this approach is failing to teach "the whole counsel of God."

2. *We must teach Bible prophecy to build the faith of believers.* As students learn how God has repeatedly kept His word in the fulfillment of Bible prophecy, their future confidence in God and the Scriptures is increased. This will make it easier for Bible study group members to trust God as they apply other Scriptures in their life. This process is described in Scripture as growing "from faith to faith,"—growing from weaker faith to stronger faith (Rom. 1:17).

3. *We must teach Bible prophecy to help our students avoid distorted teachings.* Rather than causing us to avoid teaching Bible prophecy, the abuses of prophecy should motivate us to an accurate Bible teaching ministry. A clear understanding of Bible prophecy will help your group members avoid some of the common abuses associated with prophecy. People who have never been taught Bible prophecy are more likely to be caught up in speculative interpretations than those who know what the Bible says about these matters. The fact that so many evangelical Christians are caught up in the craze of identifying dates for the return of the Lord suggests Bible teachers are not teaching the Bible or Bible prophecy as they should. If Christians knew what Jesus said about His return, they would know that "of that day and hour no one knows, not even the angels of heaven, but My Father only" (Matt. 24:36).

4. *We must teach Bible prophecy to develop Christian character.* Some avoid teaching prophecy by claiming they want to teach something more practical. Actually, the Scriptures present prophecy in a practical context to motivate us in the development of Christian character, the fulfillment of various Christian duties, and involvement in Christian ministry. Bible prophecy is the foundation upon which many of the disciplines of the Christian life are developed. The neglect of studying and teaching Bible prophecy leads to an anemic Christian life.

5. *We must teach Bible prophecy to receive the special blessing God has promised to students of prophecy.* While each of the above reasons provide good motivation for teaching Bible prophecy, this part of Scripture is so important in the mind of God that He has promised His special blessing for those who teach and study Bible prophecy: "Blessed is he who reads and those who hear the words of this prophecy, and keep those things which are written in it; for the time is near" (Rev. 1:3). You will be "blessed" when you get involved in prophecy. Those teachers who want God to bless their Bible teaching ministry must include prophecy as part of that ministry.

Narrowing the Scope of Your Study

With so much of the Bible written prophetically, the challenge of studying and teaching Bible prophecy is indeed large. As you begin studying in this area, you may want to limit the scope of your study. As you select the prophetic theme, there are several approaches you may wish to consider. You might consider the prophetic teaching concerning a particular nation or people group in Scripture, such as Egypt, Iraq (Babylon), or Iran (Persia). In another approach, you might study a particular covenant in God's prophetic plan. An example might be "the Abrahamic Covenant." A third approach might consider some specific part of the broader outline of the future, such as, "the Judgments of God," "the Crowns," "the Day of the Lord," or "the Tribulation."

As a first step in your study, gather all the biblical data available on the topic being considered. Begin by tracing the key words related to your topic through a concordance. Then consult your topic in a good topical Bible. Some publishers have produced special editions of the Bible which gather Scriptures on prophetic themes together in a topical arrangement. As you read these passages, consult the cross-references in your study Bible where your topic is mentioned. These three steps should help you uncover most of the references to your theme in Scripture.

Interpreting Prophetic Scripture

As you read and make summary notes on the contents of each passage, plan to interpret each passage literally unless there is a compelling reason not to do so. David L. Cooper has the best expression on this principle of Bible study: "When the plain sense of Scriptures makes common sense, seek no other sense; therefore, take every word at its primary, literal meaning."[1] Cooper calls this the Golden Rule of Bible Interpretation.

When God communicated His revelation to us, He used everyday words that could be understood by everyday people to whom He was speaking. In every other area of Bible study, virtually all Christians agree with Cooper's Golden Rule, but when it comes to the study of prophecy, some Christians apparently want to change the rules. They want to "spiritualize" or "allegorize" words or symbols.

Perhaps this is why there are so many abuses in the study of Bible prophecy. This problem can be corrected when we remember all Scripture, including Bible prophecy, is best understood when interpreted in its historical context using the usually accepted rules of grammar.

When interpreting prophecy, it is important to interpret each passage in harmony with the broader teaching of Bible prophecy. No prophetic statement should be taken to teach a view unique from that of other prophetic statements. Peter made this clear when he told his readers "that no prophecy of Scripture is of any private interpretation" (2 Peter 1:20).

> ### THE GOLDEN RULE OF BIBLE STUDY
>
> *When the plain sense of Scripture makes common sense, seek no other sense; therefore, take every word at its primary, literal meaning.*
> —David L. Cooper

When interpreting a specific prophecy, it is important not to separate the context from the interpretation of that prophecy. Old Testament prophecies concerning the coming of Christ may refer to either His incarnation or His second coming. Also, because of the partial nature of Old Testament prophecies (Heb. 1:1), the prophets themselves did not always distinguish between the two comings of Christ. It is possible they themselves may not have realized how much time would pass between the first and second comings of Christ.

Prophecy has been compared to descriptions of peaks in a mountain range. Two peaks may appear to be very close to our perspective, but when you get over the first peak, you find a wide valley separating the second peak which may be miles away. The same thing happens in prophecy. Two events seem very close in prophecy, but when the first event is fulfilled, the next event is separated by hundreds of years. It is not always easy to put the peaks in perspective, especially when you do not know how wide the valleys are between the peaks.

As you study, take note of specific references to the time of prediction in relationship to the time of fulfillment in the passage. Prophecy tends to switch from one extreme to another. Sometimes broad eras in history are described in general terms. At other times, the focus of prophecy deals with particular details on specific days. The references to timing in some prophecies help us distinguish the particular time period in which fulfillment should be expected. Some Old Testament prophecies were fulfilled in the crucifixion of Christ. Others may not be fulfilled until some later time such as the Great Tribulation or kingdom age. Still others may have been fulfilled in part already but a greater fulfillment remains in the future. This is called the law of double fulfillment, (Joel 2:38, 39; Acts 2:16–21). Sometimes it is not clear if the prophets themselves understand the timing of their prophecy.

Keeping your focus on the role of Christ in biblical prophecy will help prevent you from wandering down speculative paths. The central theme of all prophecy is the Lord Jesus Christ (Rev. 1:1). When the focus of our prophetic studies wanders from Christ, our view of prophecy is no longer biblical in the strictest sense of the word.

Bible prophecy should be interpreted within the historical context in which it was written. As you consider each passage in your study, ask, "What would this have meant to those who first received this prophecy?" This will help you better understand the intended message. Also, use the normal principles of grammar to guide you in your understanding of prophetic statements.

PRINCIPLES OF INTERPRETING PROPHECY

1. The primary theme and focus of prophecy is the first and second coming of the Lord Jesus Christ; however there are other themes both local and long range.
2. Prophecies are given by various means—dreams, visions, the appearance of God, the audible voice of God, internal urgings of God, and sermons.
3. Determine the historic background of the prophet when a prophecy is made.
4. Determine the meaning of proper names, events, things, geographical references, and customs that are included as part of a prophecy.
5. The way that God has fulfilled Old Testament prophecy in the New Testament is the pattern for how future prophecy will be fulfilled.
6. Separate the predictive and teaching aspects of each prophecy.
7. Look at the predictive aspects of a prophecy to determine what is fulfilled or future. Determine what is conditional or unconditional.
8. If part of a prophecy has been fulfilled in past history, let that help determine its future fulfillment.
9. Determine if the same theme or predicted event is treated elsewhere, then study them to gain light on this prophecy.
10. Determine if the prophet may treat the future as a present event, or immediately imminent, or in the distant future.
11. A future predicted event may be fulfilled in two or more steps, separated over a period of time.
12. When prophecy uses figures or metaphors, determine how the author interpreted them for your interpretation. There is usually a comparison between the thing portrayed and its interpretation.
13. Prophecy may have a multitude of facts or things, and only a few of the items are part of the coming predicted event.
14. Always accept the general principle of Scripture when you are interpreting an occurrence that seems contradictory or inconsistent.
15. Many times the prophet describes the future in light of his current cultural, social, and religious conditions.
16. No interpretation of prophecy is of "private interpretation," but should be in harmony with the general views of others in the church.

Sometimes, we need to interpret Bible prophecy according to the law of double fulfillment. This law recognizes that some prophecies may be fulfilled twice, usually once in the New Testament and again in the future. Some prophecies describe two widely separated events together. Certain messianic prophecies describe aspects of Christ's two comings together. Other prophecies may be fulfilled in a series of successive fulfillments. God's promise to judge Israel when she violates His covenant with them is an example of a prophecy with many fulfillments; Israel was judged when Jerusalem was destroyed in 586 B.C. and will be judged in the future. Still other prophecies may be fulfilled in part only to be fulfilled more fully at a later date. This appears to be true in Joel's reference to the outpouring of the Holy Spirit which was fulfilled in part on the Day of Pentecost but has a more significant fulfillment at the return of Christ (Joel 2:28–32, Acts 2:15–21). Also, some prophecies may appear to be fulfilled in the past but remain to be fulfilled in the future. Many Bible teachers see the coming of Elijah (Mal. 4:5) fulfilled in the coming of John the Baptist. Others think the passage is to be fulfilled when Elijah returns as one of the two witnesses during the Great Tribulation (Rev. 11:3–12).

The key to understanding Bible prophecy is interpreting biblical prophecy consistently. Do not keep changing your approach to various passages so you can force them into a preconceived idea. Taking that approach attempts to force the Scripture into our ideas rather than letting our ideas be shaped by Scriptures. Many Christians who keep changing their approach to fit passages into their preconceived ideas are very critical of cultic groups for doing the very same thing.

Finally, take care when interpreting figurative language so as not to read into it more than the author intended. Be careful not to read into a type more than God intended by that type. By letting the context of Scripture interpret the meaning of symbols and symbolic language, the tendency to find more than was intended can be avoided. Look for the primary meaning intended in biblical allegories and be cautious about finding other principles that were not intended by the writer.

How To Teach Bible Prophecy

Before teaching Bible prophecy, it is important that you, as a teacher, make a personal commitment to maintain balance. You should take care to avoid two extremes: first, the extreme of neglecting the teaching of prophecy; and, second, the extreme of teaching prophecy to the exclusion of other aspects of a Bible teaching ministry.

You should also strive for balance in interpreting Bible prophecy. This requires you to avoid speculating on matters that God has chosen not to make clear to us. Also, your commitment to biblical balance means you will balance your teaching of prophecy between the communication of prophetic details and the application of prophecy as a motivating force in life. God's purpose in revealing prophetic truth was not to help us design and develop new charts, but to motivate us to design and develop new *lives*.

As you begin your lesson, introduce your prophetic study in a context relevant to your students. You can do this in several ways:

- *Identify a current event that sparks interest in your study.* In a lesson dealing with the signs of the times, some event such as a famine in some part of the world may be consistent with one of the signs you will talk about that day. On other occasions, some nation or international leader may be prominent in the news and serve as an introduction to prophecies concerning that nation.

- *Identify current nations in the news with specific nations in the passage.* Many prominent nations of the Middle East, North Africa, and Eastern Europe are mentioned specifically in various prophetic passage.

- *Mention a prediction of a prominent personality.* Several times a year, supermarket tabloids feature the predictions of leading New Age gurus. The one thing each of these contemporary prophets have in common is they fail to meet the accuracy test of the Old Testament prophet (Deut. 18:20–22; 13:1–5). Their predictions may serve as an introduction to the more accurate biblical predictions being studied in your session.

As you prepare your lesson, consider alternative approaches to teaching Bible prophecy. Some teachers choose to approach prophecy topically and examine several verses from different places in Scripture to deal with a similar theme. This approach might result in a topical study on the rapture of the church. Other teachers choose to approach prophecy exegetically and examine several verses in one key passage. Using this approach might result in an exegetical study of 1 Thessalonians 4:13–18 to learn about the rapture of the church.

An ideal hostess is as careful about how food is served as about how it is prepared. Likewise, take care to teach biblical prophecy with biblical character. This can be accomplished consistently in your teaching ministry as you remember the three "be's" of teaching Bible prophecy.

1. *Be honest* in your explanations of the Scripture. Avoid making the Bible say more than it really says.

2. *Be humble* in your conclusions in prophetic interpretations. Recognize that good Bible teachers have differing opinions about prophecy.

3. *Be gracious* in your attitude toward others. Recognize that many good Christians do not share your views, and some may hold very strongly to other interpretations.

Because there are extremes and strange doctrines taught in the guise of prophecy, it is especially important that teachers are clear in their teaching of prophetic content. Many Bible teachers find charts helpful to compare similar but different aspects of prophetic themes. A chart will help students see the order of events anticipated in the future. Also, working from a clear lesson outline helps both the teacher and students to follow the lesson development. In this regard, student handouts which encourage note taking are especially helpful in teaching Bible prophecy.

When teaching Bible prophecy, remember to teach it with an emphasis on practical application in the Christian life and ministry. God revealed prophetic truth to motivate us in three closely related areas of life:

1. *Christian character.* Bible prophecy should motivate us in the development of Christian character. "And everyone who has this hope in Him purifies himself, just as He is pure" (1 John 3:3).

2. *Christian walk.* Bible prophecy should also motivate us to fulfill our Christian duties. God reveals His truth "that you would walk worthy of God who calls you into His own kingdom and glory" (1 Thess. 2:12).

3. *Christian ministry.* Bible prophecy should motivate us to accomplish significant Christian ministry. Paul taught the lesson of the rapture of the saints to the Thessalonians not to fit into a dispensational chart but to motivate them to minister to hurting people in the church. "Therefore comfort one another with these words" (1 Thess. 4:18).

Tools for Prophetic Studies

If you study and teach Bible prophecy on a regular basis, you may want to invest in a few good books dealing with prophetic themes. These books will serve as reference tools in the process of developing your studies of Bible prophecy. While not exhaustive, the following list identifies several leading books in this field. You may want to also consider some of the theology books listed in chapter 3.

Biederwolf, William E. *The Second Coming Bible.* Grand Rapids: Baker Book House, 1972.

Pentecost, J. Dwight. *Things to Come: A Study in Biblical Eschatology.* Grand Rapids: Zondervan Publishing House, 1974.

Scofield, C. I. *The Scofield Study Bible.* New York: Oxford University Press, 1909.

Walvoord, John F. *Daniel: The Key to Biblical Revelation.* Chicago: Moody Press, 1989.

———. *The Revelation of Jesus Christ.* Chicago: Moody Press, 1989.

Willmington, H. L. *The King is Coming: An Outline Study of the Last Days.* Wheaton, Ill.: Tyndale House Publishers, 1973.

BIBLE STUDY ON THE LORD'S RETURN
THESSALONIANS 4:13–17

1. What two things does Paul not want the reader to do?

   > "I do not want you to be ignorant brethren, concerning those who have fallen asleep, lest you sorrow as others who have no hope" (v. 13).

2. What has happened to those who sleep?

   > "Those who have fallen asleep" (v. 13). "Those who are asleep" (v. 15). "Our friend Lazarus sleeps, but I go that I may wake him up. Then His disciples said, 'Lord if he sleeps, he will get well.' However, Jesus spoke of his death" (John 11:11–13).

3. What two things must the reader believe?

   > "If we believe that Jesus died and rose again, even so God will bring with Him those who sleep in Jesus" (v. 14).

4. Who will go first and second when the Lord comes?

   > "For this we say to you by the word of the Lord, that we who are alive and remain until the coming of the Lord will by no means precede those who are asleep" (v. 15).

5. What three things will happen when the Lord returns?

> "For the Lord Himself will descend from heaven with a shout, with the voice of an archangel, and with the trumpet of God" (v. 16).

6. What will happen to dead Christians when the Lord returns?

> "The dead in Christ will rise first" (v. 17).

7. What three things will happen to living Christians at the Lord's return?

> "Then we who are alive and remain shall be caught up together with them in the clouds to meet the Lord in the air. And then shall we always be with the Lord" (v. 17).

8. What is the relationship between living and dead Christians?

> "The dead in Christ will rise first. Then we who are alive and remain will be caught up together with them" (v. 16, 17).

9. What positive and negative response did the writer want the readers to do?

> "I do not want you to be ignorant . . . lest you sorrow as others who have no hope" (v. 13). "Therefore, comfort one another with these words" (v. 18).

Bible Study Application

10. What happens to
    believers when
    they are "caught
    up" (v. 17)?

> *"We shall not all sleep, but we shall all be changed——in a moment, in the twinkling of an eye, at the last trumpet . . . the dead will be raised incorruptible, and we shall all be changed" (1 Cor. 15:51, 52).*

11. What should be
    the believers'
    response?

> *"We should live soberly, righteously, and godly in the present age, looking for the blessed hope and glorious appearing of our great God and savior Jesus Christ" (Titus 2:12,13).*

Bible Study Application

CHECKLIST FOR STUDYING PROPHECY

1. References
   _____

2. Does prophecy have a title/name?
   _____

3. Who gave the prophecy?
   _____

4. Place given and date given
   _____

5. What were the conditions when the prophecy was given?
   _____

6. List important words in prophecy
   _____

7. What is the context of the prophecy?
   _____

8. Who is mentioned in the prophecy?
   _____

9. Were there conditions for fulfillment?
   _____

10. Place to be fulfilled
    _____

11. Date to be fulfilled
    _____

12. What meaning does this have for today?
    _____

13. How can you apply this to your life?
    _____

PRINCIPLES OF INTERPRETATION

When you read the Bible, you want to determine what the author had in mind. This is called interpreting the Bible. When you are interpreting the Bible, you are studying it to determine the author's meaning.

Don't use a "figurative" or "spiritual" approach to interpreting the Bible. That is reading into the passage a meaning that is not there. Often this is called an "allegorical" or "figurative" way of interpreting the Bible. The reader tries to find a hidden or "deep" meaning in the Word of God. Rather, follow the normal way that normal people use when reading any book or document. Follow the literal method of interpreting the Word of God. When the Bible talks about a tree, it is describing a tree growing in a field or woods. Don't try to make a tree into a family generation or an idea that is life-giving. Follow the normal grammatical literary method of reading and interpreting literature. Follow Cooper's Golden Rule of Interpretation.

> When the plain sense of Scripture makes common sense, seek no other sense, but take every word at its primary literary meaning.

When an author uses a simile, metaphor, or other figure of speech, you will follow the rule of interpreting figures of speech—seek the meaning of the author's mind when he or she used a figure of speech, because that is what they meant. What the author means is the interpretation. Do not read into the passage an outside meaning.

When you are not sure of an interpretation, look for the meaning in other verses that discuss the same topic. Note the following principle the church has followed for over three hundred years:

> The infallible rule of interpretation of Scripture is the Scripture itself, and therefore, when there is a question about the true and full sense of any Scripture, it must be searched and known by other places (in Scripture) that speak more plainly.
>
> *Westminster Confession of Faith*

1. *Interpret the Bible in light of its historical background.* Whether you are reading prophecy, parables, or poetry, you will find the meaning of a passage when you understand the people, culture, customs, and conditions of the person(s) to whom the Scripture passage is addressed.

2. *Interpret the Bible in light of the plan and purpose.* When studying the Bible, you can better interpret it when you find out the purpose why the author wrote that portion of Scripture.

3. *Interpret a verse in light of the context of the chapter.* This means you will follow the author's thought that runs through a paragraph or chapter when determining the meaning of a particular verse.

4. *Interpret the Bible within the author's meaning of words.* The basic building blocks of language are the words that are used to communicate meaning. How an author uses words will help you find the meaning of a passage.

Understanding Words	
Etymology	Original meaning of words
Usus Loquendi	The use in a context
koine	Common meaning

When studying a Bible passage, first check the original meaning of words in a Bible dictionary. While the original use or meaning of the word may change, the root meaning will give you illustrations for teaching. You will find *usus loquendi* in a concordance. That is what it means to other people in Scripture. To find the modern usage of a word, check your English standard dictionary for its meaning.

5. *Interpret the Bible according to the rules of grammar.* Language is not a string of unrelated words like clothes hung on a line to dry. Give attention to verb tense, the match of singular and plural, and the relationship of words. To better interpret the English Bible, the interpreter must understand English grammar.

WRITING THE LESSON PLAN

The following six steps of lesson preparation should be followed by mature and beginning teachers. Each teacher will give different emphasis to each step; nevertheless, each step should be made.

1. Write the Aim

2. Arrange the Lesson in Outline

3. Write the Conclusion

4. Write the Introduction

5. Choose the Method

Sunday school teaching is not grinding out content. Nor is Sunday school teaching like a little boy playing with blocks, stacking them one upon the other in a hit-or-miss fashion. Often teaching is considered stacking blocks of content in the minds of the students. When the pile of blocks reaches its limit (the mind absorption of the student), the small boy says he is finished. The purpose of Sunday school teaching is not to communicate content only. "We teach for decisions."

Before you begin to teach, have in mind a clear decision that you want the pupil to make. This decision may be to accept Christ, to renounce a certain sin, to practice a certain behavior, or to change a certain attitude.

Try to state your aims briefly in one or two sentences. Determine what you want your student to know (mind), to feel (emotions), and to do (will).

The aim gives direction to your study. Too often, Sunday school teaching has a poor aim or none at all. When that happens, teachers aim at nothing and hit it with accuracy.

- A clear aim guides Bible study.
- A clear aim gives unity, order, and efficiency to teaching.
- A clear aim gives teachers confidence in the classroom.
- A clear aim helps teachers use time efficiently.
- A clear aim helps teachers select teaching aids and methods.
- A clear aim helps teachers evaluate a lesson.

Arrange the Lesson in Outline

Lesson preparation is not begun by writing an introduction. An introduction bridges from the student's life to the content, and the teacher must know the content before he builds the bridge. Therefore, the first step is to develop content into an organized whole. It should be sequential, building fact upon fact. Some of the following ways may be used to organize content:

1. *A series of questions becomes the lesson outline.* As either the teacher or the pupil answers each question, content is thereby filled in. A teacher should write both questions and answers in his lesson plan. If he waits to create questions until he is before his class, the right type of questions may not come. If you try to think of the answers as you stand before your students, you may be caught between home and third. Use more than one type of question. The following list may help you create a variety of questions for teaching:

   a. *Factual questions.* Usually the pupil can find the fact in the Bible or in other source material.

   b. *Interpretive questions.* The pupil is challenged to interpret a verse of Scripture.

   c. *Discussion questions.* An open-end question will bring out opinions and attitudes of pupils.

   d. *Exploration questions.* Some questions take the form of a project in which pupils are pointed to a problem and given resources for finding the answer.

   e. *Opinion questions.* At times the teacher will want to involve the pupil, by asking him to state an opinion. Why use questions?

   - To get pupils involved.
   - To motivate the student to think and study.
   - To invoke class discussion.
   - To keep students on their toes.
   - To actually teach the lesson.
   - To apply the lesson.
   - To make the transition from one point into the next topic.

2. *A series of propositional statements.* Statements are given to the class. When the students are expected to explore the Word of God to find a biblical basis. If the class is large, perhaps the teacher will have to give the statement and then explain the Scripture that furnishes the proof. Why lecture?

- To share something they don't know.
- To help them see something they can't see.
- To lift them to a level they haven't been.
- To explain passages that they can't figure out.
- To direct their thinking to issues they don't think are important.
- To expose them to teachers who have something they don't have.
- To motivate them through lethargy they can't break.

3. *List the Scripture verses with their explanation.* This is a traditional manner of Bible teaching and should not be overused by the teacher to the point of boredom.

4. *A modification or combination of the above.* The whole lesson does not have to be written out. Bible teaching is not a written speech that is read to the pupils. Try reading a speech or the quarterly and you will drive them from the study of God's Word. Be spontaneous in your presentation. Get pupils to discuss and ask questions. You should interact with them. Points in your outline should be like seeds to be sown, rather than fully blooming plants to be admired. Jesus said the Word of God was like seed sown upon the earth. Perhaps as you sow seeds in the minds of your pupils, God will bring forth a full-grown plant in their lives.

However, transition sentences should be written out in entirety. These are hinges that turn the lesson from one point to another. As you finish the introduction and move into your first point, you want to keep your pupils' interest. The introduction should capture their attention. Now keep the pupils by a smooth transition.

Write the Conclusion

Teaching without a conclusion is like fishing without a hook. The fisherman may have the best lure and equipment and be a skilled fisherman, yet if he doesn't have a hook he can't catch fish. If teaching is for decisions, then the conclusion should be designed to have pupils make a decision.

A conclusion is the aim of the Sunday school lesson applied to the life of the pupil resulting in the pupil's decision. The whole element of making a decision should be under the guidance of the teacher.

Some lessons are not concluded, they're just finished. Some teachers talk up to the final minute trying to cram in the last bit of Bible fact. Then they announce, "We'll take up here next Sunday." These teachers don't conclude—they just finish . . . finish the opportunity for God to work . . . finish their opportunity to make a change in the pupils' lives . . . and finish their greatest opportunity in life.

What about the pupil's invitation? Should the teacher in the Sunday school class give an invitation, that is, ask pupils to close their eyes, bow their heads, and raise their hands as an indication they want to receive Christ? For the most part, *no*. In small Bible classes, teachers should take the initiative to speak personally to each student about receiving Christ. If teachers don't have the courage to face pupils with the claims of Christ, they shouldn't hide behind the invitation. However, there may be times when God's Spirit works though such invitations, especially when the class is so large that the teacher cannot make a personal contact with each pupil.

A conclusion should summarize your main ideas and refresh the minds of the students. Try to get them to see the unity of the lesson.

Is it all right to have "loose ends" when you come to the end of a lesson? *Loose ends* are acceptable if they are *live ends*. "Live ends" drive the student from the classroom to seek answers and resolve issues for himself. These *live ends* are the very art of teaching. However, loose ends that leave the student confused, perplexed, and frustrated are a manifestation of poor teaching.

When coming to your conclusion, avoid letting interest lag. Do not introduce new material. You are trying to drive for a decision, and new materials may sidetrack students' thoughts. Also, do not conclude by apologizing for a poor lesson. If the lesson is poor, most students will know it; some may like it. Your apology may have introduced doubts into their thoughts about the Word of God.

The conclusion should be short, varied, real, personal, pointed, and appropriate.

Write the Introduction

The introduction is the last part of the lesson to be prepared. The purpose of an introduction is to bridge the gap from where students are to where they should be. You must prepare your lesson before you can bridge the gap from the student to that content.

A good introduction catches the attention of the pupil, creates a desire to learn, inspires him to action, and becomes a point of contact.

An introduction should promise the student something. However, like a down payment at the department store, when you promise there is more to follow, you lose your investment without the follow-through.

Types of Introductions

1. A story from everyday life.

2. A story from the Scriptures.

3. A current event illustrated by a newspaper clipping.

4. A question. For example, "Who is the tallest?"

5. A visual aid. For example, a model for junior boys.

6. An overhead transparency or slides secured from the church library.

7. A quotation from a book or significant author, such as Martin Luther.

8. A picture. For example, one that reflects the lesson to primary children.

9. A drawing on the chalkboard.

Choose the Method

The lesson plan is completed. You have planned your *materials*. Now let's give some attention to *methods*. Think in terms of two or three methods which can be used with your class. Some of the following points will guide you in choosing the method to use.

1. *Choose a method that is best suited for your lesson aim.* If your aim is to get several opinions from the Scripture passage, choose a panel discussion, debate, or forum. If your aim is to

indoctrinate, perhaps the best method is lecture or question-and-answer. If your aim is to *communicate* "feelings and attitudes," then psychodrama may be your best method.

2. *Choose a method appropriate for the age level of your students.* Do not use flannel graph with young people, as you will insult their intelligence. Also, do not try debate with primary children as they are not able to comprehend the needed logic.

3. *Choose a method that is best suited to your classroom and class size.* If there are four or five other classes in your room, you will have difficulty dividing into small buzz groups or showing a film. Also, you may have difficulty in doing a drama. Perhaps you will have to stick to lecture, question and answer, and some of the other more quiet methods. If you have a large group, then small buzz groups will enhance student interaction.

4. *Choose a method within your budget.* If your church is on a small budget, you may have to limit yourself and not use films or an overhead projector.

5. *Choose a method with variety in mind.* Lecture is an excellent way of communicating God's truth, but when used every Sunday it is overused. Variety is the spice of life, especially in teaching the Bible.

6. *Choose a method that involves your pupils.* Learning is not taking in facts but involvement with facts. Therefore, choose a method that will cause your pupils to interact with content, interact with other students, and interact with you as the teacher. The Sunday school is a place of mental gymnastics where students wrestle with the Word of God.

SAMPLE LESSON PLAN

The Person of Christ
John 21:1–14

I. OBJECTIVE

    A. Material—to analyze the spiritual state of the disciples when Christ performed His last recorded miracle on earth.

    B. To show the person of Christ can meet the need of spiritual blindness and His presence challenges us to service.

II. THE APPROACH (INTRODUCTION)

    A. How many miracles did Christ perform? Have the students guess. Explain the difference between miracles and recorded miracles. Christ performed 37 recorded miracles; we don't know how many He really performed (cf. John 20:30, 31; 21:25).

B. Use map and show the background.

> The disciples were in Jerusalem in the upper room at end of chapter 20:19, 26.

> Why did they leave Jerusalem and walk to Galilee? Matthew 28:10; Mark 16:7.

> How many miles to Galilee from Jerusalem?

III. LESSON DEVELOPMENT

A. Where is the Sea of Tiberias? John 6:1

B. Name all the disciples in verse 2. (Peter, Thomas the Twin, Nathanael, James, John, Andrew and Philip) John 1:40, 43, 44.

C. Why did Peter say, "I go a fishing?" (Note the four possible answers.)

1. Peter was the ring leader.

2. He was expressing the will of the group.

3. This was a manifestation of backsliding.

   a. They were called from their nets to follow Jesus and now they are returning. Mark 1:7.

   b. Backsliding evidenced by nothing in their nets.

4. This was a natural thing to do (go fishing).

   a. They had been living off the food supplied by Jesus (by miracles, John 6:1–14; by purchase, John 4:8).

   b. It was only natural to help out with food. "We don't go to a relative's house and eat without helping."

D. What is the result of fishing all night and catching nothing? (hungry, tired, discouraged, sleepy, depressed)—have students list.

E. Why didn't the disciples know it was Jesus? (list on chalkboard)

1. Because they were blinded due to backsliding.

   a. Mary didn't know it was Jesus. John 20:14–16.

   b. Cleopas and his wife didn't know it was Jesus. Luke 24:13–21.

   c. Unbelief brings blindness. 2 Corinthians 4:3, 4; Mark 16:11, 13, 14.

2. Because of natural conditions.

   a. They were one hundred yards from shore (length of football field).

   b. Eyes dilated because of night.

   c. Maybe fog on the lake.

   d. Early morning sun reflected on the water.

At this point, bring out the contrast that if Peter went fishing because of backsliding then the result was blindness.

List on chalkboard and point out the content.

NATURAL	BACKSLIDING
1. Fishing to help out family	1. Fishing to get away from call to the ministry
2. Caught nothing due to natural reasons	2. Caught nothing as punishment
3. Didn't recognize Christ, natural reasons	3. Didn't see Christ, blind

F. Cast nets on the right side of ship. It would have been easy to disobey a stranger; however, obedience brings blessing.

G. What is faith? Faith is obedience to the Word of God in fellowship with the Son of God. This is what the disciples did (v. 6).

H. Peter's nakedness.

Peter was not nude, but was wearing an inner garment. The coat he put on was a tunic or long, flowing outer garment to protect from sun, wind, and chilly nights.

Why did Peter put on clothes to jump into water? Most people today take off clothes when abandoning a ship. (Modest, picture of clothes of righteousness, don't know, some thought he would walk on water.)

I. Practical application, verse 7: John was the first to know it was the Lord; Peter was the first to act. Which are you?

J. This is one miracle in the count of thirty-seven. How many miracles make up the one?

(Bread, fire, fish on the fire, fish in the net, net did not break, seven not able to pull in the net, v. 6; Peter pulls in the net by himself in v. 11)

K. Why did Jesus supply miracle of fish in two ways?

(Fish on shore, was this not enough? Fish in net, was this enough?) It is a picture of God working in us, as well as without us to do His will.

L. Contrast (Have students offer the answer and list on the chalkboard.)

BEFORE WITHOUT CHRIST	AFTER WITH CHRIST
1. Lacked (caught nothing)	1. Filled —153 fish
2. Discouraged	2. Encouraged
3. Hungry	3. Filled
4. Turning back	4. Wanting to go forward
5. Didn't recognize Christ	5. Realized His presence, v. 12.

IV. APPLICATION

The lesson of "without Me you can do nothing" in John 15:5 is seen here. With Christ we can do all things (Phil. 4:13). The presence of Christ in our lives makes the difference.

V. PARTICIPATION AND METHODS OF TEACHING

A. Lecture

B. Question and answer

C. Discussion groups (buzz groups)

D. Map

E. Blackboard

ENDNOTES

Chapter 2

1. Andrew Watterson Blackwood, *Biographical Preaching for Today: The Pulpit Use of Bible Cases* (New York: Abingdon Press, 1954), 17.

2. Harington Lees, *The Joy of Bible Study* (New York: Longman, Green, 1909). Cited by Herbert Lockyer in *All the Men of the Bible* (Grand Rapids: Zondervan, 1958), 17.

3. Herbert Lockyer, *All the Men of the Bible*, pp. 11,12.

4. Andrew Blackwood, *Biographical Preaching for Today,* 36.

5. Ibid., 169-187.

Chapter 3

1. A. W. Tozer, *The Root of the Righteous* (Harrisburg, Pa.: Christian Publications, 1955), 7.

2. Gordon R. Lewis, *Decide for Yourself: A Theological Workbook* (Downers Grove, Ill.: InterVarsity Press, 1975), 9-10.

3. Philips Brooks, *Lectures on Preaching* (Grand Rapids: Zondervan Publishing House, n.d.), 129.

4. Lewis Sperry Chafer, *Systematic Theology* (Wheaton, Ill.: Victor Books, 1988), 39.

Chapter 4

1.   Merrill C. Tenney, *Galatians: The Charter of Christian Liberty* (Grand Rapids: Wm. B. Eerdmans Publishing Co., 1978), 207.
2.   Howard F. Vos, *Effective Bible Study: A Guide to Sixteen Methods* (Grand Rapids: Zondervan Publishing House, 1956), 173.
3.   Tenney, *Galatians: The Charter of Christian Liberty,* 207, 208.

Chapter 6

1.   William Evans, *The Book Method of Bible Study* (Chicago: The Bible Institute Colportage Association, 1915), 7.
2.   Merrill C. Tenney, *Galatians: The Charter of Christian Liberty* (Grand Rapids: Wm. B. Eerdmans Publishing Co., 1979), 25, 26.

Chapter 8

1.   David L. Cooper, cited by Tim LaHaye in *How to Study the Bible for Yourself* (Eugene, Ore.: Harvest House, 1976), 122.